CYBER
SAFETY

MAINTAINING MORALITY IN
A DIGITAL WORLD

SANDIE,
THANK YOU FOR
NOT GIVING UP ON
ME!

Ken Knapton

CYBER SAFETY

MAINTAINING MORALITY IN A DIGITAL WORLD

KEN KNAPTON

CFI
Springville, Utah

ISBN 13: 978-1-59955-316-0

Published by CFI, an imprint of Cedar Fort, Inc., 2373 W. 700 S., Springville, UT 84663
Distributed by Cedar Fort, Inc., www.cedarfort.com

LIBRARY OF CONGRESS CATALOGING-IN-PUBLICATION DATA

Knapton, Ken, 1967-
 Cyber safety : maintaining morality in a digital world / Ken Knapton.
    p. cm.
 ISBN 978-1-59955-316-0 (acid-free paper)
 1. Internet and family. 2. Internet and children. 3. Internet—Moral and
ethical aspects. 4. Internet—Safety measures. I. Title.

 HQ799.2.I5.K53 2009
 004.67'8—dc22

                    2009017315

Cover design by Jen Boss
Cover design © 2009 by Lyle Mortimer
Edited and typeset by Heidi Doxey

Printed in the United States of America

10 9 8 7 6 5 4 3 2 1

Printed on acid-free paper

To Debbie,
and the four technology-savvy children she brought into this digital world: Joshua, Jessica, Jacob, and Jordan.
I continue to learn from them daily.

Praise for Ken Knapton's
Cyber Safety

Ken Knapton's book, *Cyber Safety*, is an excellent resource for every parent wishing to get smart about Internet Safety. I'm a big believer in talking to your kids about their online lives and learning as much as you can about online dangers. *Cyber Safety* provides a comprehensive view of web tech in a parent-friendly format.

Marian Merritt
Internet Safety Advocate, Symantec Corporation

For those who are feeling a bit overwhelmed by the ever-changing nature of the Internet and the pervasive nature of social networks where our family members are " hanging out" with their friends, and sometimes strangers, Ken Knapton provides an insightful and practical guide to keeping families safer on the Web.

Jack W. Sunderlage
President & CEO, ContentWatch, Inc

Afraid that you can't understand the technical issues of cyber threats? This book, written by a technically savvy engineer with patents and passion in the field of internet safety, will dispel your fears. Ken explains the threats in lay terms. This is your chance to get a handle on the problem and the solutions.

Cindy Snow
Board of Directors, ContentWatch, Inc

In blending his sincere concern for youth with his impressive knowledge of computer technology, Ken Knapton has created a well-rounded, timely, and easy-to-understand resource for busy parents.

Jill C. Manning, Ph.D., LMFT
Family Therapist & Author of
What's the Big Deal about Pornography?:
A Guide for the Internet Generation

As a parent advocate and author, I see this book as an excellent tool and resource for parents who want to learn what is lingering in cyberspace, which is now today's playground for not only our children, but also for those that have less than moral thoughts and behavior. This book offers analogies that even a parent without a lot of technology exposure will be able to understand. When your child's real life becomes part of a digital life, you need to be educated and you need to be a step ahead, which can be impossible with the ever-changing World Wide Web. You owe it to your children to read this book to help you and them better understand what is lurking online.

Sue Scheff
Parent Advocate, SueScheff.com

Written with precision and detail, this book doesn't leave any room for confusion about Internet Safety. Ken outlines real-life examples that all family members need to know before going online.

Alan Fullmer
Founder, CEO, ZooBuh.com

Knapton makes complex technical concepts easy to understand and has specific recommendations for how families can protect themselves from the shadowy parts of the Internet. If you want some help, this is a great place to start.

Joel Dehlin
CIO, LDS Church

CONTENTS

FOREWORD

As president of iKeepSafe.org, I have a vision of seeing generations of the world's children grow up safely using technology and the Internet. I have many opportunities to meet with parents and educators, policy and thought leaders, as well as industry businessmen, and the more I discuss issues of cyber safety with them, the more timely Ken Knapton's message becomes. I am convinced that every home and every parent must engage in this issue. Cyber safety is no longer a topic that can be left to the techno-geeks and IT experts. Technical solutions alone won't prepare our youth to be responsible and resilient Web users. Every child needs the active involvement of a caring parent.

The good news is you don't have to be a computer expert to keep your child safe online: a little learning goes a long way. Every parent can learn those essential skills, and *Cyber Safety* will guide parents through this process. The emerging risks associated with all connected technologies (e.g., Internet, cell phones, game consoles) include three primary risks: inappropriate contact, content, and conduct.

- **Inappropriate Contact:** Teach children that people aren't always who they say they are online or in a game. They should also be able to recognize and protect themselves from contact with cyber-bullies, hackers, phishers, and predators.
- **Inappropriate Content:** Teach children to keep away from content that doesn't meet your family's standards. (Filtering and monitoring will help you establish those standards.) This includes both content that is viewed and content that is created and uploaded by them. Help them understand that everything they

post online is tracked and stored (cached) and will follow them to future job interviews, or even bishop's interviews.

- **Inappropriate Conduct:** Teach children that the Internet is a public forum, and that their conduct can be traced back to them. Help them understand that everything they post online contributes to the digital reputation that will follow them into the future. Help them create an online reputation that is an asset rather than a liability.

Given these risks, iKeepSafe recommends three general guidelines for keeping children safe online: keep current, keep communicating, and keep checking.

- **Keep current** with the technology your child uses. You don't have to be an expert, but a little understanding goes a long way toward keeping your child safe online. Get basic technical training and learn about new products as they're released.
- **Keep communicating** with your children about everything they experience on the Internet. Ask questions about the three risks. Know with whom your child is communicating. Know their lingo and ask when you don't understand something. Work to keep communication lines open.
- **Keep checking** your children's Internet activity. Use filters and monitoring software. Let them know that you'll keep checking because you want them to understand that the Internet is a public forum and never truly private.

In the chapters that follow, Ken Knapton provides an excellent foundation for understanding the risks and for following through with safety measures. He presents the underpinnings of the Internet in terms that anyone can understand and provides a foundation upon which parents can build a solid understanding of the digital world.

Cyber Safety will help parents implement safety and security in the technologies used within their homes. As Knapton explains the dangers, he offers pragmatic solutions in each chapter for what we as parents can do, right now, to keep our families safe online. He explains how children can bypass the tools put in place by their parents, exposing themselves and their equipment to serious risks. And he outlines the warning signs of this risky behavior.

Cyber Safety gives parents a tool kit for helping their children become responsible digital citizens. It is my hope that as parents and communities work together, we can help children become ethical, responsible, and resilient cyber-citizens who are able to respond to any situation they encounter online. The concepts provided in this book offer a solid foundation for reaching this goal.

Marsali Hancock,
President, iKeepSafe.org

INTRODUCTION:
THE DIGITAL AGE

"100 years ago, people still traveled by horse and buggy. The age of the telephone and electricity was just dawning. There was no air travel, no Email, no fax machines, no Internet. There has been an explosion of secular knowledge. I believe that God has opened up these treasures of intelligence to enhance His purposes on the earth. The new century will bring exponential advances in that treasury."[1]

James E. Faust, 1999

It is a very different world from the one I grew up in. I was raised in a small town in New Hampshire which, I believe, to this day still doesn't have a fast food restaurant or a movie theater. Everyone knew each other, and it was a rare occurrence to run into a stranger in town. If someone saw me walking down the street with an adult that they did not recognize, they would ask me who the adult was and what I was doing with them. My world was very small, and it would have been very difficult for a predator to come into our little town and abscond with any children.

Of course, this small town environment also inhibited access to inappropriate material for youngsters. If we were hanging around the magazine stand a little too long, which back then was the only place to access such material, someone would notice, and I could be certain that my mother would later ask me what magazines I'd been looking at. Everyone knew me, everyone knew my family, and the community did not hesitate to communicate about such matters.

It is a different world today. The world is much larger, and information is much more available. It is estimated that in one week of reading the New York Times, a person encounters more information than was available in

1

an entire lifetime in the eighteenth century. It has been estimated that more new information will be generated this year than was generated in the past five thousand years.[2]

Let me be very upfront about my biases. I have spent my career working in the high tech industry, and I believe that technology is a key part of life today. It is not going away; it is not a fad. And trying to shield our children from it would do them more harm than good. While this book is not intended to be a religious work, it is important to understand that I believe that this explosion of technology has been given to us by God, and that there is a very specific reason that He needs this technology to be available on the earth today. Raising morally righteous children in this technological world brings with it new challenges. Instilling in and maintaining for our children a moral standard in today's world is more difficult than it was in years past, not because there are any new sins or new ways to offend God, but rather because those age-old temptations are now much more available to us and to our children.

Throughout history, any time something good is given to us by the Lord, it is corrupted for evil uses by the adversary. So it is with technology today. This book is not a religious reference, nor is it intended only for those who believe that there is a higher purpose behind the technology we have today. Rather it is a helpful reference book for anyone trying to instill a moral compass in their children and in their family, and for anyone trying to keep their family safe from the online dangers that surround us. It is intended to help de-mystify the technology we have in our homes, and bridge the gap between my generation, the digital immigrants, and the digital natives—our children.

Because the Internet is an unregulated, collaborative space, we really have no control over all of the information that is distributed by it. New content is posted to the Internet every day by people all over the world. Content spans from teaching people how to tie knots to bomb-making instructions, and from pictures of a recent family reunion to hard-core pornography.

Unfortunately, this means that in today's digital world, access to inappropriate, hurtful content and dangerous predators are as close as our family computer. As parents, we cannot simply allow our children to wander the Internet without some sort of supervision or control, but our control also needs to account for appropriate use of this wonderful technology that puts the world at our fingertips. There is so much good stuff out there that we really don't want to throw the baby out with the bathwater. It is not realistic to simply turn off the Internet to our homes. Our children are going to access the Web somewhere, whether that be at a friend's home, at our local library, at Internet cafés, or at school. There is great benefit to encouraging our children to access the Internet to complete their homework assignments, stay in touch with friends, or to keep up with politics, sports, and other worthwhile interests. The Internet will play an increasingly important role in our children's lives, and keeping them away from it would, in my opinion, do them a disservice when it comes time for them to find employment in this digital world.

Nevertheless, we cannot be naïve about the real dangers lurking on the World Wide Web. The first section of this book is intended to highlight these dangers by discussing some of the problems that have come about with the increased popularity of the Internet. Some recent estimates indicate that as much as *half* of the content on the Internet is pornographic in nature, or at the very least, it is intended only for adult consumption. Our laws have yet to catch up to the technology, and, unfortunately, this content is not appropriately limited in a way that keeps it from our children.

Apart from the danger of running across inappropriate content, there is also a very real danger of becoming a victim of a child predator. In section 1, we learn of a study done by the FBI that shows that anyone who spends any significant amount of time in chat rooms has a 100 percent chance of interacting with a predator. Our children don't understand this danger so it is up to us, as parents, to help them understand and avoid the dangerous dark alleys of the Internet. We all teach our children about "stranger danger" and how to avoid getting abducted from the mall or during their walk home from school, but for some reason, we let our guard down when it comes to their online interactions with complete strangers. At the very least, it is our responsibility to protect our children from such dangers, even if it means curbing their freedom to explore.

As we will see a little later in section 1, we shouldn't hold our collective breath waiting for legislation to fix this problem. There are some complex legal issues at play that will take many years to sort out—if they ever are. Responsible parents need to watch over their children's online activities in much the same way they watch them in the mall, at the park, or in any other public place.

Some people may argue that vigilantly supervising our children's online activities violates their right to privacy. The truth is, however, that allowing our children to wander the Internet freely because we don't want to invade their privacy is analogous to allowing our children to wander around a large city unaccompanied because we don't want to inhibit their freedom of choice. They could find their way to a museum or a movie theater, or they could end up in a very bad part of town. The virtual world of the Internet is even more insidious. Our children don't need look for the dangerous areas of the Internet; even if they don't search it out, they will come across some type of pornographic content if they spend any significant amount of time online. If they frequent chat rooms, they will encounter a predator, and if they spend time on social networking sites the chances are high that at some point they will experience some form of cyber bullying. As responsible parents, we cannot sit back and do nothing; we must help them navigate the Web appropriately.

When the television was introduced, many people raised concerns that television would erode family communication and relationships because parents might use it as a babysitter and would not interact with their children as much as they did before owning a television. The potential for parental neglect and familial disassociation are legitimate concerns with television media; however, the potential for these problems exponentially increases with the Internet. Our children spend more time using digitally connected technology today, and they do it with much less supervision, than they ever did watching television. To make matters worse, most parents are essentially blind to the subtle, eroding effects of the Internet.

Among the things we will discuss in this book are the very real dangers of social networking sites and their effects on our children's behaviors. This phenomenon has created an environment where perfect strangers sometimes know more about our children and their worries and concerns than we, their parents, do. For example, the Australian Broadcasting Corporation recently published a news story regarding the Internet and its effect on teenagers—especially those who participate in online social networks. The news story raised an interesting question: When children are struggling or in trouble, how do we, as parents, find these early warning signs that are so easily seen by their peers online? In the smaller world of yesteryear, these warning signs would usually make their way back to us as our children's friends would confide in their parents and those parents would, in turn, communicate with us. Today, this loop does not exist. Those in whom our children confide may be thousands of miles away, with no link to our family unit. Understanding social networking technology and how our children use it is key to learning more about our children and keeping them safe. As parents, few of us would allow our children to go to a party without asking some basic questions: "Where is it?" "Who will be there?" "What parents will be in attendance?" "How old are the other children who will be there?" and so forth. Yet when it comes to the Internet, we take a completely different approach: they can go anywhere, do anything, and talk to anyone, without our involvement or oversight—mainly due to our lack of understanding about the technology.

One proactive way to manage Internet usage in our homes is through the use of content filters. In addition to reviewing the effects of social networking sites on children's behaviors, the Australian Broadcasting Corporation's news story also discussed how easily children can bypass filters—most technically-savvy children can. The role of filters today is misunderstood by many parents; or, more appropriately stated, parents today expect too much from filters. Filtering technology is primarily written to keep unwanted content off of our computers; that is, it is written to "keep honest people honest." However, if someone wants to get around the filter, it certainly can be done. It is important to remember that no technology is good enough for parents to install it once and then ignore their children's Internet usage forever. A filter should not be used as a replacement for involvement in our children's online activities, but rather, it should be just another tool that we use to help us be more involved in what our children are doing online. A filter is a very good start, but don't allow yourself to fall into the trap of believing that because you have installed a filter, your work of protecting your children online is done. As parents, we need to provide the Internet tools and rules that will help our children have good experiences online, and avoid the bad stuff out there. Additionally, we need to understand what our children are doing online—what social networks they a part of, what blogs they actively participate in, and whom they talk to.

At first glance, this task may seem daunting, if not overwhelming. It is possible, but, as parents, we need to educate ourselves and understand how the technology works—not at a deep technical level, but deep enough that we know what our computers are being used for and how we can prevent them from being misused. We need to know when someone is trying to hide his computer usage, or when our children may be trying to pull the wool over our eyes.

That is the reason for this book. This book attempts to lay out the technical underpinnings of the Internet in a way that anyone can understand, whether you have a technical background or not. Once you understand how content is spread across the globe via the communication super-high-way, you can then understand how technology can help you protect your family—and you can understand the limitations of technology [3] and where you need to step in.

The truth is that it is not an issue solely of technology but of parenting in a new, digital world. I hope you enjoy this book and that it can provide some insight on the digital technology your children already understand.

Notes
1. James E. Faust, "This is Our Day." *Ensign*, May 1999, 17.
2. www.ShiftHappens.org
3. For a variety of reasons, not the least of which is the fast-moving world of software development, I will refrain from recommending many specific software solutions in this book. However, if you are not certain of where to find these applications, you can always perform a simple search using your favorite search engine (Yahoo!, Google, Ask, or any other). Specify the type of software you are looking for (i.e., anti-virus, anti-spyware), and you can usually find something fairly quickly. As of the writing of this book, there are several free applications available (simply add the word *free* to your search criteria to find these), as well as many professionally maintained and updated versions for purchase.

SECTION 1

THE PROBLEM

1
PORNOGRAPHY

"The plague of pornography is swirling about us as never before. Pornography brings a vicious wake of immorality, broken homes, and broken lives. Pornography will sap spiritual strength to endure. Pornography is much like quicksand. You can become so easily trapped and overcome as soon as you step into it that you do not realize the severe danger. Most likely you will need assistance to get out of the quicksand of pornography. But how much better it is never to step into it. I plead with you to be careful and cautious."[1]

Joseph B. Wirthlin

It is a sad fact that the "adult entertainment" industry (which is just a politically correct way to refer to the pornography industry) has been the driving force behind many of the advances in in-home content delivery. It was this industry that drove the acceptance and popularity of VCRs in the 1970s and 1980s, as evidenced by a study released in 1980 that indicated that 60 percent of video sales in the United States were for pornographic use. [2] The adult entertainment industry also spurred acceptance of cable television, and this trend continues with the Internet today. It is very difficult to determine exactly how much pornography is currently available on the Internet, but recent studies estimate that 12 percent of the total websites in existence are pornographic in nature.[3]

The Scope of the Problem
In an effort to understand just how large that number is, and to see how difficult it is to actually track this problem, we need to estimate the

size of the Internet. While no one actually knows its exact size, it can be estimated based on the number of registered domain names. A domain name is a primary address, and there is one for every location on the Web. Domain names must be centrally registered in order to function as a real address. (We will discuss domain names in more detail in Chapter 6).

This chart shows the growth of Internet domain names since 1994,[4] which is just about the full life of the Internet to date. Keep in mind that this just tracks domain names, not the myriad of individual pages that could reside at each address. A domain can have many, even hundreds or thousands, of individual web pages behind it. Think of MySpace.com or facebook.com—single domains with thousands of actual web pages that make up their sites. As a matter of fact, if MySpace were a country, it would be the 11th largest country

	Registered Domain Names
1994	—
1998	50,000,000.00
2000	100,000,000.00
2002	175,000,000.00
2004	250,000,000.00
2006	400,000,000.00
2009	650,000,000.00

in the world, right between Japan and Mexico.[5] And that is only one domain name on this chart. So we can start to see how difficult it is to get a handle on the actual size of the Internet.

Using the data from this chart and making the assumption that each domain averages at least five pages (which is an extremely conservative estimate), it is safe to say that there are well over 3.25 billion pages on the Internet today—and it is still growing. Taking this very conservative number and multiplying it by that 12 percent estimate brings us to about 390 million pornographic pages to encounter on the Internet.[6] Regardless of the study or calculations used, it is safe to say that around half a billion pornographic websites exist today, just waiting for our children to find them.

And finding pornography on the Internet is not difficult. InternetFilterReview.com reports that 25 percent of all daily searches on the Internet are for pornography—this equates to 68 million daily searches! They also report that 90 percent of eight- to sixteen-year-olds have viewed pornography online, usually while doing homework.[7] With that much illicit content just sitting out there, it is clear that whether they search for it or not, anyone who spends time on the Internet is going to stumble across this content unless measures are put in place to prevent that from happening.

According to the CP80 foundation, which was established to combat the problem of pornography on the Internet, if a child were to look at one pornographic web page every ten seconds, he would be 296,443 years old by the time he looked at every adult-oriented web page on the Internet in 2007.[8] It is also important to note that all of these estimates include only the actual web pages that contain pornographic images. That is to say, it does not include the individual images or video files that are shared via Internet technologies such as email or peer-to-peer file sharing (which we will discuss in greater detail in Chapters 9 and 10). In other words, there is an immense amount of pornographic content available over the Internet today—and it is growing at an alarming rate.

> Our estimate puts the number of pornographic web pages at 400,000,000. If every pornographic web page was printed and piled up together, the stack of pornography would be over 15 miles high.
>
> www.cp80.org

PORNOGRAPHY AS A BUSINESS

The pornography industry is not to be underestimated. It is much larger than most people realize. In fact, it is one of the largest industries in the world, with an estimated $97 billion in annual revenues worldwide.[9] Pornography generates more money on an annual basis than most sports, television shows, or other entertainment industries. For example, in the United States alone, the porn industry generated more annual revenue than the television networks of ABC, CBS, and NBC combined. It is not a small industry.

As with any industry, simply having a lot of content is not enough to keep the business thriving. The purveyors of this content have aggressive marketing campaigns and do everything possible to get their content in front of potential buyers. The sad truth is that the Internet has provided fertile ground for growing their business. The World Wide Web creates an environment where we no longer need to go searching for this adult content. It now comes directly to us, often when we are not even seeking it.

In his DVD presentation entitled "Standards Night Live," popular speaker and author John Bytheway uses the example of the evolution of weapons targeting systems as an analogy to describe this phenomenon. Many years ago, it took thousands of bombs in order to completely destroy a target. The problem was that these bombs were only accurate to within thousands of feet, so they would have to send plenty of them to ensure that the target was destroyed, which also caused plenty of "collateral damage." Over time, as the technology used to guide these missiles improved, accuracy was also greatly improved, and now a single bomb can be deployed from an aircraft and then guided through the door of the intended target, with little or no collateral damage. John then goes on to describe how the availability of pornography has gone through a similar transition. Many years ago you had to venture out to an adult book store or video shop to find this adult-oriented material (i.e., thousands of feet). Soon, much of this material made it to your corner store (hundreds of feet). Today, we do not even need to venture out of our home to find this content—it is available within the walls of our own homes. This analogy is quite accurate; all of the content on the Internet is available from the comfort of our own homes with just a few clicks of the mouse.

The Internet also provides a mechanism for much more targeted marketing efforts and allows companies to target those efforts to a very specific demographic for extremely little cost. In the pre-Internet days, companies had to print advertisements and mail them to your home. Today, they can simply place content on the Internet where you would easily stumble upon it, or they could spam it directly to your email inbox. Both of these methods carry very limited cost since there is nothing to print out and no cost for mailing. Unfortunately, the pornography industry views most of the population as part of their demographic and target their efforts to everyone with an Internet connection.

Obviously, their marketing methodologies work very well. Recent studies have shown that 40 million people are "sexually involved" over the Internet[10] and that the average age of first exposure to sexually explicit content on the Internet is 11 years old.[11] We already learned that 90 percent of children have been exposed to inappropriate content on the Internet while doing research for their homework. The Crimes against Children Research Center has reported that 1 in 5 teenagers who regularly log onto the Internet have received a sexual solicitation via the Web.[12] Sex, pornography, and the Internet are tightly intertwined, and the problem is growing exponentially.

Years ago, we were warned of drug dealers who lurked around schools and provided free drugs to children. Once children experimented with their free dose, they would be hooked and the dealer then had a steady clientele. Studies have shown a similar addiction from viewing pornography. In a DVD entitled "Pornography: The Great Lie," the Utah Coalition against Pornography discusses how the porn industry has followed a similar business model to the drug dealers of old. Some people go to work every day with the express intent of getting their pornographic content in front of as many people as possible—free of charge. They know this content to be highly addictive and are doing everything in their power to get it in front of anyone who could be drawn in and eventually pay for more of that content. The Internet has given them a perfect venue for such activities. No longer do they need to convince people to trudge down to the local corner store to purchase adult materials—they simply need to get them to turn on their computers.

Anonymity magnifies the problem

The lure of anonymity has made this content available without social stigma. No longer do people need to be concerned about neighbors recognizing them, or noticing the mailman delivering an embarrassing magazine. Instead, they can sit at their computer, in the privacy of their own homes, and consume as much of this content as they like. The problem is that the same content is also available to everyone else who accesses the Internet—including our children.

There was a time when the only risk of a child viewing pornographic material at home was if a parent brought it into the home in the first place. Purchase of the material was limited to adults, so we could easily dismiss a child's exposure to the material as his parent's fault for leaving adult content where he could find it. Today, however, simply connecting a computer to the Internet makes it possible for this content to come into the home, without parental knowledge, consent, or approval. The parent's only fault is connecting the computer to the Internet and leaving the access unprotected.

The Internet is indeed a very dangerous place. It is not a family-friendly environment. And yet, children know more about it, and are more familiar with it, than their parents. After all, they are the digital natives—they grew up with this technology. Parents are the digital immigrants, needing to learn about this new technological world. So, what is a parent to do? While some have simply decided not to allow the Internet in their homes, this does not completely solve the problem. Our families have access to the Internet at friends' homes, school, the library, work, cyber cafés, and many other places. Throwing our hands up or sticking our heads in the sand does no good. We need to educate ourselves about what content our children are viewing—whether they seek it out or it is forced upon them. The more we know about the Internet and its dangers, the better armed we are to have an intelligent conversation with our children. Only then will we be able to effectively combat the problem of pornography on the Internet.

What To Do

- ➢ If you don't have a filter, install one. We will discuss filters and how to choose the best filtering solution for your family in Chapter 6.
- ➢ Review the reports from your filter often.
- ➢ Most filters have the ability to notify you when something is blocked or when someone views something that is against your usage policy. Use this feature, and talk to your children when you receive these notifications.

Notes

1. Joseph B. Wirthlin, "Press On," *Liahona*, Nov. 2004, 101–04.
2. http://www.medialit.org/reading_room/article260.html.
3. http://www.internet-filter-review.toptenreviews.com/internet-pornography-statistics.html.
4. Data for this chart is as reported by the Internet Systems Consortium "Domain Survey," http://www.isc.org/solutions/survey.
5. www.ShiftHappens.org.
6. http://www.internet-filter-review.toptenreviews.com/internet-pornography-statistics.html.
7. Ibid.
8. The CP80 Foundation, 2007.
9. http://www.internt-filter-review.toptenreviews.com/internet-pornography-statistics.html.
10. Internet Porn Statistics: 2003, http://healthymind.com/s-porn-stats.html.
11. Internet Filter Review, Internet Pornography Statistics,

http://www.internt-filter-review.toptenreviews.com/internet-
pornography-statistics.html.

12. http://www.ojp.usdoj.gov/ovc.publications/bulletins/internet_
2_2001/internet_2_01_6.html.

2
INTERNET PREDATORS

"There is nothing in the scriptures, there is nothing in what we publish, there is nothing in what we believe or teach that gives license to parents or anyone else to neglect or abuse or molest our own or anyone else's children. . . . There is in the scriptures, there is in what we publish, there is in what we believe, there is in what we teach, counsel, commandments, even warnings that we are to protect, to love, to care for, and to 'teach [children] to walk in the ways of truth'. To betray them is utterly unthinkable."[1]

Boyd K. Packer

ALICIA KOZAKIEWICZ

On October 17, 2007 CBS News ran a story[2] about nineteen-year-old Alicia Kozakiewicz.[3] When Alicia was thirteen years old she was chatting online with someone she thought was a fourteen-year-old girl. They became friends and talked about all the things they had in common. The friend knew all of the lingo, slang, clothes, styles, and everything else that she needed to know to make Alicia feel comfortable and believe that her online friend was indeed a fourteen-year-old girl. They decided to meet, but instead of a finding a friend, Alicia found herself abducted by Scott Tyree, a pedophile who took her across state lines and tortured her for four days. Scott posted images online of Alicia being tortured, which led to someone reporting the incident and, eventually, to her rescue. Alicia now spends her time traveling the country to talk about Internet safety. In testimony before congress in 2007 she said, "The boogey man is real. And he lives on the Net. He lived in my computer—and he lives in yours . . . While you are sitting here, he is at home with your children." Alicia is one of the lucky ones. Many of these cases end up like Christina Long, who was found strangled to death in 2002.[4] While her case is still open today, the police believe that she was killed by someone she met online.

The statistics regarding Internet predators are just as scary as those regarding pornography on the Internet. According to a survey done in 2000 by the National Center for Missing and Exploited Children and the Justice Department, one in every five children ages ten to seventeen said they have received a sexual solicitation over the Internet. The FBI has also released a study in which they state that anyone who "frequents chat rooms" on the Internet has a 100 percent chance of interacting with an Internet predator.[5] WiredSafety.org reports that one in four U.S. teen girls has admitted to an in-person meeting of someone they met online, while one in five U.S. teen boys admit the same.[6] While not all of these led to a meeting with a predator, they certainly all had the potential for a very poor outcome. Bear in mind that all of those individuals who have been molested by an Internet predator went willingly to meet their abductor.

It is a sad fact that there are many, many stories like those of Alicia and Christina. The global nature of the Internet, coupled with the trusting nature of children, make for a deadly combination. The vast majority of these stories do not end happily. Fortunately, there are usually plenty of warning signs—parents just need to know how to find them. Predators will spend quite a bit of time developing a relationship of trust with their victim—sometimes up to several months or even years—before ever meeting them in person. The preferred method of interaction is either chat rooms or instant messaging applications (possibly embedded in a social network). Many of these chat sessions quickly dive into extremely graphic sexual content. A simple review of chat or instant messaging logs, both of which can be monitored relatively easily using current technology, would reveal any items of concern and prevent possible tragedy.

> **The boogey man is real. And he lives on the Net. He lived in my computer —and he lives in yours. . . . While you are sitting here, he is at home with your children.**
>
> **Alicia Kozakiewicz**

The main problem is, once again, either a fear or ignorance of the technology that can be used to monitor activity on the Internet; or, worse yet, a parent who doesn't want to infringe on the privacy of his children. We would not allow our children to walk into a bar at one o'clock in the morning. Why do we allow them to chat on the Internet at all hours of the night? Why does it seem that we are infringing on their rights when we watch what they do on the Internet, but it doesn't seem like infringing on their rights to stop them from walking into the middle of a busy street? The world is changing, and there are very real dangers in the virtual world. We need to be as vigilant in protecting our children from the digital dangers as we are about protecting them from the physical dangers.

PREDATORS AND CHILDREN'S WEBSITES

The Internet is full of predators. Whenever I speak on this topic, people inevitably tell me that their children are not at risk because they are only allowed to go to children's sites. This is like saying that your children are safe from predators because you only allow them to go to the mall with their friends. Recall the story of Adam Walsh, the son of John Walsh (host of *America's Most Wanted*) who was abducted from a mall in Florida and killed in 1981. Adam was in the mall with his parents when he disappeared, abducted in the light of day from a busy store in the mall. In those days, predators would hang out in malls, near playgrounds, or near schools, searching for their victims. They knew where children would be, and they went there in search of those children.

Today, things are not much different. Internet predators often lurk on sites that attract children. Predators know how to find their victims—they know where they hang out on the Internet, and they know the right jargon, as evidenced by Alicia's story. The truth is that they don't have to look very far for their victims. The Internet is really a world-wide playground— anyone can enter and anyone can hang out anywhere they like. Predators are not going to spend their time on adult sites; they are going to spend their time where children are. Some of them have commented, after being caught, that the popularity of social networking sites has only made their job easier. They use the instant trust level inherent in these sites to groom their victims over time.

The unfortunate truth is that although these reputable sites attempt to verify that only children have access, there is no viable way to determine the true age of the individual sitting at the keyboard. Internet predators are going to go where the kids are and they then blend in with the children on that site. So limiting your children's Internet access to kids' sites does not remove them from danger. Remember, there are no "set it and forget it" solutions when it comes to the Internet. Even if you limit your child's access to only child-friendly sites, you still must be vigilant regarding his Internet usage.

CATCHING PREDATORS

I recently heard Mark Shurtleff, Attorney General for the State of Utah, speak on this subject. He mentioned that Utah's Internet Task Force has had a 100 percent conviction rate for the past three years. This task force has not been kept secret—their arrests and successes have been published and documented for all to see. He commented on how surprised he is that predators still troll the chat rooms and try to lure children to meet with them when they know there is a significant possibility that they are actually interacting with a police officer. Even with all of the attention on this subject, much of it brought about by the "To Catch a Predator" series on *Dateline*, the problem is not going away. The addiction and the draw is just too strong for those who want to do harm to our children.

The reason predators continue to use this medium is that our children love to chat on the Internet. All of their friends are online, and most are involved in some type of social networking or gaming site where they meet new people every day. As hard as these websites try (and I am not convinced that many of them are really trying), there is no valid mechanism to determine the age of any individual in a chat session. Our children love to gather online, but allowing them to do so unmonitored is like letting them walk down a dark alley in the worst part of town on any given night. The danger is simply too great. Therefore, parents must be especially vigilant.

WHAT TO DO

➢ Know what your children are doing online. Make an effort to know where they spend their time and whom they chat with. Talk to them and take Ronald Reagan's advice to "trust, but verify." Use technology to monitor their chat sessions and watch for warning signs of predatory interactions.

➢ Review their social networking sites. Have them add you as a friend so you can monitor their pages and posts. Log onto their social networks regularly, check their home pages, and watch for posts from their friends. Remember that it is not snooping if it is posted on a social networking site. It is out there for anyone to read—so read it!

> Install monitoring software to log their chat and instant messaging conversations and then review the logs on a regular basis. There are plenty of applications that can monitor these conversations, and they are very easy to install and use. Find one, install it, and monitor it regularly, watching for warning signs of predators.

Notes

1. Boyd K. Packer, "Children," *Liahona*, Jul 2002, 7-10.
2. CBS News, Fighting to Hunt Predators Online, October 17, 2007, http://www.cbsnews.com/storyies/2007/10/17/eveningnews/main3379003.shtml.
3. For more on Alicia, see http://www.zimbio.com/Alicia+Kozakiewicz/.
4. 60 Minutes II, June 25, 2003. http://www.cbsnews.com/stories/2002/09/23/60II/main523017.shtml.
5. www.ContentWatch.com
6. http://www.wiredsafety.org/internet_predators/index.html.

3
CYBER BULLYING

"Sometimes hurts to the heart are more damaging than physical blows."[1]

Marvin J. Ashton

MEGAN MEIER AND RYAN HALLIGAN

Cyber bullying is a relatively new form of harassment that is accomplished using technology. One of the strangest cases of cyber bullying is found in the sad story of Megan Meier.[2] Megan was a thirteen-year-old girl, who had a MySpace page that she used to keep in touch with her friends. She was not the most outgoing of teenagers, and, like many other girls her age, she suffered from low self-esteem. So when a sixteen-year-old boy befriended her on MySpace, she took to the relationship quite quickly. He was cute and wanted to be her friend. He said his name was Josh Evans and that she hadn't met him in school because he had just moved to town and was home-schooled. Nonetheless, he said he lived in the neighborhood and he wanted to be her friend.

They never met in person, and Josh told her that he didn't have a cell phone, so the only communication they could have was online. Only six weeks after becoming friends, Josh started posting hurtful messages about Megan online, not just to her but on pages where everyone could read it. He would post insulting comments about her weight and make derogatory comments about her. Megan was confused, and extremely upset over the strange turn the relationship had taken—she could not understand where this had come from and why the friendship had taken such a sudden turn for the worse.

On October 16, 2006, she received her final message from Josh. It said, "Everybody in O'Fallon knows how you are. You are a bad person and everybody hates you. Have a sh***y rest of your life. The world would be a better place without you."[3] After reading this message, Megan went upstairs to her bedroom and hung herself in her closet. She died the following day.

In a strange twist to this disturbing story, it turns out that Josh Evans didn't even exist—he was a fictitious person, made up by the parents of one of Megan's friends with whom she'd had a falling out. Yes, these were adults posing as a young boy with their only intention being to embarrass and harass this young, thirteen-year-old girl. This is the epitome of what is now known as cyber bullying.

Unfortunately, Megan's is not a unique story. Ryan Halligan was a thirteen-year-old boy who committed suicide after being bullied at school and online.[4] It wasn't until after his death on October 7, 2003 that his father found some transcripts of instant messaging conversations that he had been having, which showed the cyber bullying.

WHAT IS CYBER BULLYING?

Cyber bullying is becoming a big problem on the Internet. CyberBullying.org defines it as follows: "Cyber bullying involves the use of information and communication technologies to support deliberate, repeated, and hostile behavior by an individual or group, that is intended to harm others."[5] Normally, the term *cyber bully* refers to a young child harassing another child, but the phenomenon is not limited to our children. When similar things happen to adults, it is usually referred to as *cyber harassment* rather than *cyber bullying*, but it has the same hurtful and dangerous effects in the end. Both terms involve using technology—the Internet, email, cell phones, and so on—to harass or embarrass an individual on a repeated basis.

Since this is a relatively new problem, not much research has been conducted on this topic. However, the United States Health Resources and Services Administration reports the following statistics from the few studies that have been done:[6]

+ 18 percent of students in grades 6–8 said they had been cyber bullied at least once in the last couple of months and 6 percent said it had happened to them 2 or more times.

+ 11 percent of students in grades 6–8 said they had cyber bullied another person at least once in the last couple of months, and 2 percent said they had done it two or more times.

+ 19 percent of regular Internet users between the ages of 10 and 17 reported being involved in online aggression; 15 percent had been aggressors, and 7 percent had been targets (3 percent were both aggressors and targets).

+ 17 percent of 6–11-year-olds and 36 percent of 12–17-year-olds reported that someone said threatening or embarrassing things about them through email, instant messages, websites, chat rooms, or text messages.

+ Cyber bullying has increased in recent years. In nationally representative surveys of 10–17-year-olds, twice as many children and youth indicated that they had been victims and perpetrators of online harassment in 2005 compared with 1999–2000.

Other research shows that most youth who are victims of cyber bullying tend to keep it to themselves, although pre-teens are more apt to inform someone than teenagers are. StopBullyingNow.com reports:

+ 51 percent of preteens but only 35 percent of teens who had been cyber bullied had told their parents about their experience.

+ 27 percent of preteens and only 9 percent of teens who had been cyber bullied had told a teacher.

+ 44 percent of preteens and 72 percent of teens who had been cyber bullied had told a friend.

+ 31 percent of preteens and 35 percent of teens who had been cyber bullied had told a brother or sister.

+ 16 percent of preteens and teens who had been cyber bullied had told no one.

WHAT TO DO

Megan Meier's parents thought they were doing everything right with regard to her online activities. They monitored her time online, kept a close eye on her MySpace friends, and watched what she posted to her page. Although their daughter told them of the hurtful messages, they had no idea how dangerous those messages were. Ryan Halligan's father, on the other hand, was shocked when he read the instant messages on his sons computer after his son's death. While Mr. Halligan was aware of the physical bullying that was happening at school, he had no idea that this same thing was happening online. Had he known about these conversations sooner and had Megan's parents understood the devastation that the hurtful messages were causing their daughter, maybe these tragedies could have been avoided.

So what can we as parents do to uncover cyber bullies? Here are a few suggestions:

1. Keep watch over your children's instant messaging and email conversations, as well as their cell phone text messages. Children will be hesitant to bring these problems to the attention of their parents, but adults can usually tell if something is not right in the tone of a conversation. While this may seem like an invasion of privacy, the computers and cell phones are yours, and you have the right and responsibility to ensure your children's safety while using them. Inform your children that you will periodically check these communications so they don't feel betrayed when you come to them about something you noticed in one of their conversations.

2. Talk to your children about their online friends. Ask them often about their conversations and how they feel about their online relationships. Watch for sudden changes in these relationships.

3. Since children tend to tell their friends before they tell an adult, talk to your children about "bystander" rules—if they know of someone who is being bullied online, they need to tell an adult, and to encourage their friends to do so as well.

4. Periodically search your children's names to see what is being posted about them online. You can do this on Google, Yahoo!, or any other common search engine. Also, check their social networks for posts about them and remember to search for their name or nicknames as well.

5. Watch for the warning signs: if your children become angry after spending time online, if they withdraw, if their grades suddenly decline, if they suddenly change their attitudes about school, if they get sick more often and remain home from school, or if they change their habits regarding their friends, take note. These are all possible warning signs of online cyber bullying.

Cyber bullying is a very dangerous and concerning problem. Because of the anonymity that accompanies online personas, it is easy for people to get carried away and say hurtful things through technological means that they would most likely never say in person. If you are watchful and stay interested in your children's online interactions, cyber bullying can be detected and resolved very quickly, before any long-term harm is done.

Notes
1. Marvin J. Ashton, "While They Are Waiting," *Ensign*, May 1988, 62.
2. http://abcnews.go.com/GMA/story?id=3882520&page=1.
3. http://meganmeierfoundation.org/story.
4. http://www.ryanpatrickhalligan.org.
5. http://www.cyberbullying.org.
6. http://www.bullyingresources.org/main/adult/indexAdult/asp?Area=cyberbullying.

4
MALICIOUS SOFTWARE

"Not all stealing is at gunpoint or by dark of night. Some theft is by deception, where the thief manipulates the confidence of his victim."[1]

Dallin H. Oaks

As the use of technology increases, so does the risk of exposing our critical data. We use the computer to keep track of our finances and to store critical pieces of information such as social security numbers, passwords, login information for our financial institutions, and so forth. In the physical world, we protect this data by locking it in a drawer, hiding it in a can on the shelf, or maybe storing it under our beds. We try to secure it by keeping it out of view—a methodology known as "security by obscurity." The virtual equivalent might be to simply hide this data in a file that is named something innocuous, like "recipes" or "movies I want to see." Unfortunately, technology has advanced enough that this type of "security by obscurity" is completely useless against today's high tech criminals. We have technology that can search the content of documents without regard for the file name or where it is hidden on the computer. Many of these applications have been written for law enforcement so they can find evidence that criminals have tried to hide (and those criminals will use much more sophisticated means of hiding their evidence than a typical computer user would). The problem is that criminals have access to this same software and can find anything they want on any computer they can gain access to. These criminals are also getting smarter with regard to how they obtain access to our data—even tricking us into willingly providing that data to them so they don't have to come searching for it.

Malicious software is the term used to describe applications that are written with the express purpose of gathering, exposing, or doing harm to your data. There are many different types of malicious software today, ranging from mild to severe. These can be used to steal identities, steal money, or simply destroy or corrupt your data. Let's explore a few of the reasons that you need to be aware of malicious software.

IDENTITY THEFT

Software that is created for the express purpose of retrieving or exposing personal data is considered a type of malicious software. Those who obtain this data usually either use it themselves to steal your identity or sell the data to others who will steal your identity. Identity theft is an increasingly common crime in the United States. In early 2008, the United States Department of Justice cited the following as recent cases of Identity Theft: [2]

- Central District of California. A woman pleaded guilty to federal charges of using a stolen Social Security number to obtain thousands of dollars in credit and then filing for bankruptcy in the name of her victim. More recently, a man was indicted, pleaded guilty to federal charges and was sentenced to 27 months' imprisonment for obtaining private bank account information about an insurance company's policyholders and using that information to deposit $764,000 in counterfeit checks into a bank account he established.
- Southern District of Florida. A woman was indicted and pleaded guilty to federal charges involving her obtaining a fraudulent driver's license in the name of the victim, using the license to withdraw more than $13,000 from the victim's bank account, and obtaining five department store credit cards in the victim's name and charging approximately $4,000 on those cards.
- District of Kansas. A defendant pleaded guilty to conspiracy, odometer fraud, and mail fraud for operating an odometer "rollback" scheme on used cars. The defendant used false and assumed identities, including the identities of deceased persons, to obtain false identification documents and fraudulent car titles.

There is a very real danger of identity theft when using the Internet. Phishing scams, where the criminal will set up a website to look just like a site we trust and then try to direct us to it and convince us to enter our personal data, is a very popular, and successful, mechanism for obtaining our critical data. Email and peer-to-peer file sharing applications are also used to spread malicious code directly to our machines. These codes then either gain access to our data or log keystrokes and send them to the thief. Most of our teenagers use email and file sharing applications on a very regular basis. Unless we educate ourselves about the real dangers surrounding the use of these applications and convey to our children how to avoid those dangers, we are playing right into the hands of the criminals who want to get our data. As with any other criminal activity, the perpetrators will always look for the path of least resistance, which means that even very small effort on our part could go a long way toward preventing the theft of our data.

VIRUSES

Another form of malicious software is software that is simply designed to cause harm to your data by erasing it, corrupting it, or making it unusable for your purposes. Some of these criminals are motivated by nothing more than the notoriety that accompanies a successful, large-scale attack, but far more are motivated by a desire to steal our date for their financial gain. This is usually accomplished by writing a computer virus and getting it to replicate itself to other computers via the Internet. The virus may be replicated by accessing your address book and sending an email to all of your friends, by attaching itself to a file that is being shared from your computer via a peer-to-peer application, or by any number of other replication mechanisms. Some viruses are even starting to propagate themselves via the popular social networks that our children use today. The mere fact that your computer is connected to the Internet gives these viruses the opening they need to quickly replicate themselves on other computers.

Of course, most perpetrators have realized that the Web provides a far easier way to spread their code than disks or simple manual file sharing, and these harmful applications are now being written to automatically send spam to all of your contacts in an attempt to get them to enter credit card numbers into a malicious website, or to install a keylogger that will gather their usernames and passwords to websites and send them on to the perpetrator of the worm or virus. While notoriety is nice, making money is even better—and the virus writers are becoming more intelligent in how they can monetize their worms and viruses.

To better understand the magnitude of the problems that come from malicious software, we will review some of the latest data available as of the writing of this book. The following information is found in the Internet Threat Security Report, Volume XIV, dated April 2009, published by Symantec Corporation.[3]

According to the report, the number of active malicious code threats is steadily rising year over year, as seen in the chart below. As you can see, the incidents of malicious code are growing at alarming rates. Amazingly, 60 percent of the malicious code detected was discovered in 2008, which means that the majority of the malicious code is due to new attacks, rather than a proliferation of attacks from prior years. These new attacks average out to 28.7 million detections per month in 2008. Over 90 percent of those attacks are threats to our confidential data.

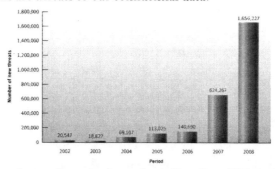

Source: Symantec Corporation, Internet Security Threat Report XIV, April 2009

There is a very real underground economy for this stolen data, and criminals can make a very lucrative living if they can steal enough data. As you can see from this chart, there is an associated price for every piece of personal data that they can harvest from our machines, or that they can convince us to enter on a website that they operate.

2008 Rank	2007 Rank	Item	2008 Percentage	2007 Percentage	Range of Prices
1	1	Credit card information	32%	21%	$0.06–$30
2	2	Bank account credentials	19%	17%	$10–$1000
3	9	Email accounts	5%	4%	$0.10–$100
4	3	Email addresses	5%	6%	$0.33/MB–$100/MB
5	12	Proxies	4%	3%	$0.16–$20
6	4	Full identity	4%	6%	$0.70–$60
7	6	Mailers	3%	5%	$2–$40
8	5	Cash out	3%	5%	8%–50% or flat rate of $200–$2000 per item
9	17	Shell scripts	3%	2%	$2–$20
10	8	Scams	3%	5%	$3–$40/week for hosting, $2–$20 design

Source: Symantec Corporation, Internet Security Threat Report XIV, April 2009

Web-based attacks were the most popular mechanism for attack in 2008, as can be seen in the following chart. A web-based attack is where the attackers will either re-create a well known website on their own server and then try to get us to visit that site instead of the real one (this technique is known as phishing) or they will compromise a high-traffic website through a vulnerability specific to either the website itself or an application running on the site. They will then siphon off data that they are interested in that we have provided to that website.

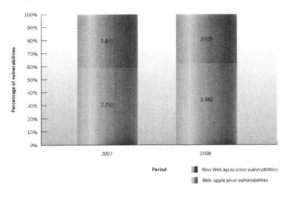

The report also finds that more than ever before hackers are now using their skills for their own financial gain, as seen in the following chart. The most active sector for phishing attacks was the financial sector: banks, credit unions, credit card companies, and other online financial institutions. Hackers are getting much smarter about how they attempt to trick us, preying on our level of trust in our financial institutions coupled with our lack of understanding about Internet technologies. These things make it easy for criminals to steal the financial data that we willingly enter on those types of websites, and they then use this information to drain our bank accounts. According to the report, the most popular data for sale on the underground economy servers in 2008 was credit card data, which is most likely due to the fact that there are numerous ways for credit card numbers to be stolen, and it is also easy for these cards to then be cashed out.

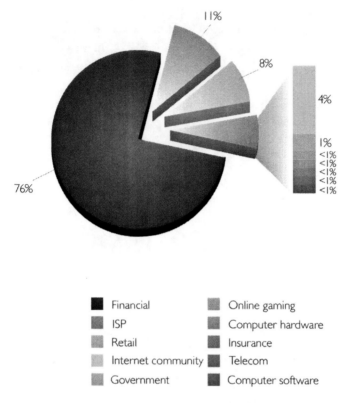

11%

8%

4%

1%
<1%
<1%
<1%
<1%
<1%

76%

■ Financial	■ Online gaming
■ ISP	■ Computer hardware
■ Retail	■ Insurance
■ Internet community	■ Telecom
■ Government	■ Computer software

Figure 2. Phished sectors by volume of phishing lures
Source: Symantec Corporation

While web-based attacks are now the most common method of infection, that does not mean that the only way to get infected by a virus is to surf the Web and be tricked into entering your information on a phishing site. There are many ways that malicious software can infect our computers via web-enabled technologies. The criminals who write this software find very creative ways to entice people to run applications that include a malicious payload. There are several mechanisms for the criminals to use, ranging from convincing you to run an application attached to an email message (Hey, watch this really funny video!) to simply asking you for the information (An email arrives in your inbox, apparently from the IRS. It informs you that you are going to be audited, and instructs you to reply with some specific personal information). The key is that you have to act in some way to provide them with the information they want. Most viruses are propagated when the operator of the computer takes some action that initiates the unwanted activity written into the virus. The good news is that viruses can't spread without our help. The bad news is that we are either so gullible, curious, or trusting as human beings that the spread of viruses continues to grow year after year.

Symantec reports that the primary method of infecting computers with malicious code is through file sharing executables, which are applications that exist on removable media (such as USB drives, memory sticks, floppy disks, and other shared media) and propagate themselves when these media are shared from one computer to another. Email attachments are another popular method of infection, as well as peer-to-peer applications. (We will discuss email attachments and peer-to-peer file sharing in more detail in chapters 9 and 10.) The following chart shows some of Symantec's findings regarding the different propagation mechanisms in use as of the writing of this book:

2008 Rank	Propagation Mechanism	2008 Percentage	2007 Percentage
1	File-sharing executables	66%	44%
2	File transfer/email attachment	31%	32%
3	File transfer/CIFS	30%	26%
4	Remotely exploitable vulnerability	12%	15%
5	File sharing/P2P	10%	17%
6	File transfer/embedded HTTP URI/Yahoo! Instant Messenger	4%	3%
7	SQL	3%	3%
8	Back door/Kuang2	3%	3%
9	Back door/SubSeven	3%	3%
10	File transfer/Yahoo! Instant Messenger	2%	1%

Source: Symantec Corporation, Internet Security Threat Report XIV, April 2009

SPYWARE

One other form of malicious software is called *Spyware*. This is software that is placed on your computer for the express intent of sharing your personal information with others, almost always without your knowledge or permission. This could range from cookies that simply remember what websites you visit and send that data back to their host when requested, to full-blown applications that run on your computer and periodically send data to some location on the Internet. They may record your keystrokes, watch for passwords, or worse yet, watch for combinations of web addresses, usernames, and passwords, such as what you would use to access your online banking. If your machine slows down over time, it is possible that you have spyware of some sort running. As more spyware loads and runs in the background on your computer, these processes take more time slices from your CPU, thereby slowing down your machine. Spyware can be propagated in the same way that viruses can—that is, by email, peer-to-peer file sharing applications, or simply surfing the Web and downloading. Some websites propagate spyware by dropping cookies onto your machine; however, they can also download and install themselves during other activities, such as when your children are playing a game on a website. Once you give permission for a website to download a video or game to your machine, just about anything can then be installed. Essentially, you have opened the door—anything can walk right in without making you aware of its presence.

WHAT TO DO

It is a sad fact of life that there are people who want to use technology to do us harm. They actively search for ways to access our computers and exploit critical data. The soaring popularity of the Internet, which brings with it ever-increasing bandwidth and home computers that are always connected to the Internet, provides a breeding ground for this malicious software.

Fortunately, in this case, the virtual world is much like the physical one. Anything that we can do to slow down these criminals usually causes them to leave us alone as they search for the path of least resistance. In the physical world, we know that something as simple as leaving our house lights on deters criminals and causes them to move to a home with no lights. Making use of security software to protect our computers is like leaving our lights on or installing a deadbolt on our front door. Just as we would not think of leaving our home unlocked, likewise we should not consider accessing the Internet without some level of protection in place.

Similarly, every Internet-connected computer should have, at the very least, a firewall (i.e., the deadbolt), an anti-virus application, and an anti-spyware application (considered our virtual "lights"). These should be configured to update themselves from their publisher on a regular basis, and every so often, a full scan should be performed. Performing these scans will keep your computer running smoothly and will reduce the risk of losing critical data. There are ways to schedule automatic scans that run when the computer will be idle, so it doesn't interfere with your normal usage. Review your software manual to see if it offers this type of setting (most do). If it doesn't, most standard operating systems have scheduling capabilities.

Finally, one side note regarding anti-virus and anti-spyware applications: under normal circumstances, you do not need more than one anti-virus application installed on your machine. Choose one that you like, make sure it remains updated, and leave it running. Installing more than one anti-virus application normally serves no purpose, other than to slow down your machine. Anti-spyware protection, on the other hand, can benefit from more than one application. Each anti-spyware application vendor looks for different things, and no one application available today cleans off all of the spyware that is on your computer. Personally, I have two anti-spyware applications installed on my machines, and I run scans in both of them about twice a month.

Keeping your computer running smoothly is much like maintaining your car. In order to maintain peak performance, you need to perform regular maintenance. Run regular anti-virus and anti-spyware scans on your computer just as you would change the oil in your car. As previously mentioned, most of these applications allow you to schedule scans for hours when the computer is not in use. Make use of this capability and sleep better knowing that your computer and your data are protected.

Notes

1. Dallin H. Oaks, "'Brother's Keeper'," *Ensign*, Nov. 1986, 20.
2. http://www.usdoj.gov/criminal/fraud/websites/idtheft.html, Feb. 2008.
3. This information is available publicly at http://www.symantec.com/business/theme.jsp?themeid=threatreport. Excerpts and charts reprinted here by permission.

5
LEGISLATING THE INTERNET

"The only thing necessary for the triumph of evil is for good men to do nothing."[1]

Edmund Burke

HISTORY OF CHILD PROTECTION LAWS ON THE INTERNET

Many people wonder why we don't just pass laws to protect our children from the dangers of the Internet. Indeed, many new laws have been passed in an attempt to solve, or at least slow, the problems incident to the Internet. For example, prior to 1998 it was not illegal to steal another person's identity. In fact, in one of the first identity theft cases, the suspect actually contacted the victim to tell them what they had done and boasted that there was no recourse for the victim since it was not yet illegal. Laws have now been passed that make it illegal to steal another person's identity and, as we have learned in Chapter 4, people are now successfully prosecuted for it.

Sadly, when it comes to legislation, it is easier to protect our data than our children. This is especially true of pornography. It has not been as easy to create anti-pornography laws that can withstand judicial review as it was to create anti-identity theft laws. In recent years in the United States there have been several attempts to impose legislative restrictions on Internet content; however, most have failed. On the national level, the Children's Online Privacy Protection Act (COPPA)[2] was passed in 1998, but was almost immediately restricted from being enforced by an injunction in the court system. Since then, COPPA has ping-ponged between the Supreme

Court and the district court and has been, essentially, unenforceable. In 2004 the case was again remanded for further review based on one of the findings of the Supreme Court that "filter's superiority to COPA is confirmed by the explicit findings of the Commission on Child Online Protection, which Congress created to evaluate the relative merits of different means of restricting minors' ability to gain access to harmful materials on the internet."[3] In other words, filtering technology had improved so much since 1998 that there may now be a "less restrictive" means to accomplish the same task, so the Supreme Court remanded the case back to the district court to investigate this theory. As of the writing of this book, the case is again awaiting a hearing at the Third Circuit.[4] It is expected to be overturned and thrown out for good. In the meantime, many states have attempted similar laws, with similar results.

Other attempts have been made at the national level, including the Communications Decency Act of 1996, which was struck down due to a lack of nationwide community standard to measure against, and the Children's Internet Protection Act of 2000, which requires libraries and public schools that receive certain funding to provide filtered Internet access. Although this law remains in effect, it was watered down considerably by the United States Supreme court's decision (U.S. v American Library Association, 539 U.S. 194 [2003]) which required that a library disable its filter for any adult patron who requests it, regardless of their reason for wanting unfiltered access. There are also plenty of libraries that simply do not request the funds tied to this law so that they will not have to abide by its dictates.

As of the writing of this book, the Utah legislature is planning to debate a new bill (Utah house Bill 139)[5] which proposes that an ISP be held accountable if a minor who accesses the Internet via their service encounters material intended for adults. While the intent of the legislation is to be admired, the fact remains that it is extremely difficult to author legislation that protects our children on the Internet while still passing the first amendment bar. The main problem that this bill faces is the same problem that all other legislative efforts in this area face: how to let adults who want to access pornographic material do so while not allowing our children the same access. As per the Supreme Courts findings, as long as there are less restrictive means to accomplish the same task, the court system will continue to strike down these laws.

In lay terms, this essentially means that as long as there are filters which people can install if they want to, we will not be able to legislate the availability of this content on the Web since filters are always a less restrictive means to achieve the same goal. There may be some possibility for the Utah law to pass, since it targets public Internet connections which children can access from anywhere. However, in this author's opinion, if this law passes, all it will do is reduce the number of free, wireless hotspots, as the providers will not want to assume the liability associated with it. It is almost impossible to legally stop someone from accessing pornography if they really want to do so, and it is certainly extremely difficult to determine if the person accessing the pornography is of legal age to do so or not. Internet service providers know this, so rather than accept the liability, they will simply close down their hotspots.

PORNOGRAPHY AND THE FIRST AMENDMENT

To be clear, I am of the opinion that it is more important to protect our children from unintentionally accessing this material than it is to maintain easy to access for adults. Personally, I don't believe that the first amendment requires that adult material has to be "easy" to access at all. As adults, those who really want to view this material can jump through a hoop or two if it means preventing innocent children from accidental exposure. But the courts don't seem to see it that way—at least according to recent rulings on the matter.

In the physical world, restricting access to pornographic material is really not a difficult problem. We can put adult material in the back room and restrict access to it or we can place covers on magazine racks so kids (or anyone else who doesn't want this forced on them) can be protected from inadvertent exposure to this material while standing in line at the local grocery store. Several states have passed laws to this effect, and they remain intact and fully enforceable.

In the virtual world, however, it becomes a more difficult problem from a legal standpoint. There is no real equivalent of magazine covers on the Internet. The closest thing was the attempt a few years ago to require a warning page with a link that said something like "only adults are allowed to see this. If you are an adult, click here to gain access" (which was a result of COPPA). While this does prevent accidental exposure, it does nothing for the curious youth who is happy to lie about being an adult just to see what is behind the curtain. The current legal interpretation of the first amendment has left us in a situation where we now have to try to create legislation that protects children while still allowing adults to get anything they want on the Internet without having to slow down for virtual speed bumps we may want to put in the road—very difficult to do.

TECHNICAL HURDLES TO SUCCESSFUL LEGISLATION

The technical problems to be overcome are not small. For example, there is no way to accurately and definitively determine someone's age over the Internet. Legislation requiring people to enter credit card information to access adult content was shot down because it made too many people nervous about entering their information and was deemed a violation of free speech. Moreover, it excluded adults without credit cards from the adult Internet community. Another problem with a credit card entry system is that there is no guarantee that it is actually an adult who enters the credit card number. These days, many children can easily find a parent's credit card number. Until we have a way to determine that the person on the other end of the connection is 18 (or 21) years old, there will be no reliable method of age verification over the Internet.

To make legislation even more difficult, the Internet is a world-wide entity (thus the "www"—*World Wide* Web) and is not bound by the laws of any one country. This makes it extremely difficult to legislate the Internet since those who want to continue to offer their content will simply move their servers outside of the state or country where the law is in effect to protect themselves from prosecution. Given the worldwide nature of the Web, I would not hold my breath for legislation to solve the problems that our children face while using the Internet.

EDUCATION IN ADDITION TO LEGISLATION

While I support COPPA, the Utah house bill, and others like it, I truly believe that this is not a legislative problem. Just like many would argue that we need to teach abstinence in school rather than handing out condoms, likewise we need to instill our children with a moral compass that will help guide them as they wander the virtual world of the Internet. Occasionally, they will experience something that we would rather they didn't. Unfortunately, that is a fact of life. Even with filters installed, our children may occasionally encounter images that we prefer they do not see. But if we teach them to use their moral compass, they will quickly be on their way and shun the illicit content that makes its way into their lives via the Internet.

While there are some laws and technology that can help, the most effective way of protecting our children on the Internet is through a societal and educational solution—not a technical or legislative one. Although the purpose of this book is to provide some insights into the technological tools that exist today and to help parents who may not be technically savvy to be able to use those tools, the bottom line is that as parents, we need to change our behaviors regarding how we monitor and manage the technology that our children use, or these problems will never go away. The problem is not inherent in technology; it is in how we manage and oversee that technology within the walls of our own homes.

Notes

1. M. Russell Ballard, "Let Our Voices Be Heard," *Ensign*, Nov. 2003, 16, quoting from John Bartlett, comp, *Familiar Quotations,* 15th ed. 1980, ix.
2. http://www.ftc.gov/ogc/coppal.htm.
3. http://supct.law.cornell.edu/supct/html/03-218.ZS.html.
4. As part of this case, this author was deposed and provided testimony regarding the technology that currently drives filter products. Many readers will also recall that it was in relation to this case that Google refused to comply with a court order regarding its search data, which made headlines for several weeks. Eventually, Google did provide the requested data.
5. http:/le.utah/gov/~2008/bills/hbillint/hb0139.htm.

SECTION 2

TECHNOLOGIES AND SOLUTIONS

6
UNDERSTANDING THE INTERNET

"This is an age of wonders. It is an age of scientific miracles. The computer, the Internet, email, and a hundred other things pertaining to communication have added to our ability to speak to one another with speed and ease."[1]

Gordon B. Hinckley

Before we can discuss the methods for protecting your family, we need to have a quick lesson on how the Internet works. This chapter is a small diversion from the Internet Safety topics that the rest of the book is focused on, and is written in more of a lesson format. It may feel more like a textbook chapter for classroom instruction—but it is necessary to lay a foundation upon which we can build in the rest of this book.

I attempt to present these topics in a very easy-to-understand way, and to explain the very technical underpinnings of the Internet in plain language, not tech-speak. In doing so, many details are left out—this is intentional. The goals here are to lay that foundation and to provide some insights into ways in which you can quickly determine how your computer is being used. The more you understand about how the Internet works, the better equipped you will be to keep your family safe from its dangers. The technical details that are missing from this explanation have little relevance to the issues we will discuss. If you already understand the Internet and know the technologies used, I only ask that you put on your "mother-in-law" hat, and view this chapter through the lens of a techno-phobic, non-computer-geek.

THE INTERNET

By way of definition, the Internet is the connection mechanism by which many different computers can provide, find, and share information. This includes many different technologies, including transmission technology (called protocols) that power such applications as email, web browsing, file sharing, and others. When you use a browser to locate a website, you are usually using a portion of the Internet called the World Wide Web (which is where the "www" in most internet addresses comes from). For the purposes of this chapter, we will focus mainly on this portion of the Internet—the part that is used to surf websites using a browser. Other technologies (that is, other protocols) will be introduced in later chapters.

Just as locations in the physical world are identified by addresses, so virtual locations on the World Wide Web are also identified by addresses. It is not by coincidence that the virtual addresses of the Internet are constructed in much the same way as addresses in the physical world. For example, when you address a letter in the physical world, you can send it from anywhere in the globe, and there is enough information on that letter for it to be routed to the desired location. The address is globally unique. It includes the country, state, street, apartment number (if needed), and the name of the intended recipient.

The Internet is very similar. The address for a web location is called a Universal Resource Locator, or URL for short. Similar to a physical address, a URL is globally unique; that is, it points to a single entity on the Internet, no matter where you are geographically located.

Although there are similarities in physical and virtual addressing, there are a couple of distinct differences. For example, the Internet has no concept of zoning laws. In the physical world (at least in the United States) we have zoning laws to keep a manufacturing plant from being built next to your house, or to prohibit a strip mall from being built across the street from a city dump. The Internet has no such rules, and predators and pornographers take full advantage of that fact. One wrong turn could take you into a world completely different from where you thought you were going, and there will be no warning signs that you are headed into a bad part of town, virtually speaking.

One major difference between an Internet address and an address in the physical world is that an address on the Internet does not have any inherent geographical relevance. That is, you cannot always tell by reading the URL whether the content it contains is housed in the United States of

America, or Japan, or anywhere in between. Often, even visiting the URL provides no hints as to where the content is being hosted. As you surf the Internet, you literally span the globe. From one click of the mouse to the next, you could view content from anywhere in the world, with no indication as to where the content is coming from.[3]

This makes for a very different experience than we are used to in the physical world. Normally we have some visual indicators of our geographical whereabouts—a map, some street signs, or other clues that provide geographic context. The Internet has no such clues, nor is it relevant (most of the time). However, there are ways to understand what type of site is sending us the content, even if we can't tell where it is originating. We will learn about some of these later in this chapter.

INTERNET DELIVERY MECHANISMS

Now let's discuss how content is delivered to and from Internet addresses. When you connect to the Internet, your computer is assigned an address.[4] When you surf the Internet, you are simply contacting different addresses on the Internet and asking them to send content from their address to yours. Just as letters and packages (i.e., content) can be delivered in the physical world from one address to another, so web content is delivered between two addresses in the virtual world.

Think for a moment of the myriad of ways to get content into your home in the physical world. You could receive a letter or package via the United States Postal Service, UPS, Fed-Ex, or some other delivery company. If the package is over a certain weight limit, it may be sent to your home using a different delivery service: such as the delivery arm of a furniture store, or it could be sent via DHL or a moving company. Or, when you are moving furniture from one home to another, the delivery mechanism could be a bunch of your friends with trucks—it doesn't have to be a formal delivery service. The same holds true on the Internet.

Because we do not understand the virtual delivery mechanisms of the Internet, we tend to be more trusting and allow just about anything into our homes—often thinking that it is okay because we have installed a filter to protect us or that since we have an anti-virus application installed, our data can't be harmed. Unfortunately, this is far from the truth. Allowing different delivery mechanisms (i.e., protocols) into our home without regard for what they do is even more dangerous in the virtual world than it would be in the physical one. Although the delivery mechanism is virtual, the content that is transported via that mechanism is very real and can be just as harmful to us as a stranger with a weapon entering our home. And yet, because of our misunderstanding of technology, we are more lackadaisical in protecting our homes from these virtual intruders. We will delve more into this concept as we conclude this chapter.

Just as there are different delivery mechanisms in the physical world, there are corollaries in the virtual world. The delivery mechanisms that operate in the virtual world of the Internet are called "protocols." Like the delivery services in the physical world, different protocols are used to transport different types of data. In the virtual world you can receive content through a browser (HTTP or HTTPS), as an attachment to an email (SMTP or POP), a file-sharing application (each application has its own protocols), or a direct file transfer (FTP or SFTP).[5] A protocol can be thought of as a way of delivering content to your home, much like the United States Postal Service (USPS), UPS, Fed-Ex and the others we spoke of above.

Just like each delivery service in the physical world has its own rules and regulations,[6] there are many different rules for the protocols on the Internet. This means that virtual content is addressed and sent to the computer in your home based on very specific addressing rules and delivery regulations.

There are many ways for content to be delivered to your home in the physical world—some that you trust and other that are more suspect. If a stranger were to knock on your door and request to deliver a couch that you did not purchase, you would probably not allow him into your home. If he then showed you a receipt with the signature of someone you trust (such as a parent or spouse), you would then be more likely to allow him into your home to complete the delivery.

Protocols on the Internet are the same—they each have different restrictions and security concerns. Some are secure and can be trusted; others are less restrictive and require more scrutiny. Additionally, some protocols can be screened by online filters and others cannot be filtered at all. (We will dive into the concepts of filtering in Chapter 7.) The Internet is not just one technology, but rather it is an entire virtual world, with several different delivery mechanisms made up of various technologies. In order to protect our children, we need to understand the differences between and know what is available via each of these different mechanisms, and we need to be clear about the possible dangers of each.

Decoding Internet Addresses

While it is usually impossible to know exactly where Internet content originated geographically, it is possible to get some idea of where it came from simply by looking at its address. This section explains how websites are identified on the Internet and how URLs are defined. Regardless of the delivery protocol, all content is delivered to a URL.

While the real address of any location on the Internet is actually an Internet Protocol (IP) address (i.e., 10.1.1.5), we don't usually enter these when we are trying to navigate the Internet. This is because it is much easier to remember the name of a site (its "domain name") than it is to remember some seemingly random number. However, either is valid. If you were to enter the letters www.google.com in your web browser it would take you to the same location as entering the site's IP address (which as of the writing of this book is 74.125.19.147).[7] Go ahead, try it. Just type the IP address into your browser and see that it takes you to Google. Both addresses are exactly the same as far as the Internet is concerned, and both take you to the same location. As a matter of fact, the URL is the actual addressing mechanism used by the Internet—the Domain Name is just an alias that we humans use to interact with the Internet. Aside from being easier to remember, domain names also provide more flexibility for site providers, since site IP address may change. By using domain names, no one needs to know when a site's IP address changes. The site owners simply point their domain name to the new IP address, and no one is the wiser.

Internet addresses, or domain names, consist of a Domain, Subdomain and a Top Level Domain (or TLD). The address is usually preceded by the *protocol* to be used to send the content. Thus, the address is organized as follows:

protocol://SubDomain.Domain.TopLevelDomain

For example: http://www.google.com

Entering the above address informs the browser to use the Hyper-Text Transmission Protocol (HTTP) to send you the content from the designated domain. A domain is the basic element of an Internet address. Every URL must point to a domain, which is the virtual "building" where all of the content for that site is housed. When you set up a website, the first thing you do is register the domain name. This is usually the name of your company, like Disney or AmericanAirlines.

The Top Level Domain (TLD) is usually a three or four character suffix that indicates what the domain refers to. For example, ".com" is sup-posed to refer to a company, ".gov" should be a government site, ".edu" is an educational institution, and so forth. The TLD should give you an indica-tion of what type of site the URL points to, without having to actually visit the site. TLDs are predefined by the Internet Consortium, and are limited to only those TLDs that have been approved for use by them. Therefore, you could not create a web address with a custom TLD, such as .myname because it would not be valid in the Internet community (yet).

TLDs are as important to a Web address as "avenue," "street" or "bou-levard" are to a physical address. In other words, "1600 Pennsylvania Avenue" is a different physical location than "1600 Pennsylvania Street." Similarly, WhiteHouse.com and WhiteHouse.gov are two very different sites, operated by completely different entities. One is a business named "WhiteHouse" (which, as of the writing of this book is a search site) and the other is the official government entity representing the building the President of the United States lives in. Just as people sometimes arrive at the wrong physical location because they have confused "street" with "avenue," they can also arrive at the wrong Inter-net address by entering the wrong TLD. There was a time when "white-house.com" was a porno-graphic site. This was done intentionally to catch people who were trying to get to white-house.gov, but mistyped the TLD. This used to be a common tactic used by purveyors of pornography and is still a very popular phishing technique, even though new regulations now make the practice of deliberately misdi-recting URLs illegal.

At one time there was a suggestion that the Internet Consortium approve a ".xxx" TLD for the express purpose of hosting adult content. The reasoning was that such a TLD would make it easier for parents to filter out this content, since all they would have to do is block every site that uses this TLD. The Internet Consortium declined to approve this, however, due to concerns that there would be no way to force all adult

Continuing our analogy, if the domain is the building and the TLD is the street name then the subdomain is the apartment number. It points to a specific location within a domain. The subdomain only has validity within the confines of the domain, much like an apartment number only has valid-ity within the confines of the building that houses it. Consequently, subdo-mains can be used over and over again with different domain names. For example, "images.google.com" and "images.yahoo.com" point to different locations. Both are image sub-sections of two competing search engines. Think of the housewares section of Target and of Walmart—different domains (Target and Walmart) with the same subdomain (housewares). They have similar types of content, but a different provider and ultimately different content.

While an Internet address may only have one domain, it can have multiple subdomains and multiple TLDs. For example, it is very common for a second TLD to indicate the country code for a site, as follows:

http://cars.images.searchme.com.cn

This URL indicates that a search company (searchme.com), which is located in Canada (.cn) has some content where you could search for images (images.) of automobiles (cars.), which would be delivered to your browser (http).

When you understand how internet addresses are built, you can see how people use minor variations on a URL to collect personal information or direct you to content that you did not intend to invite into your home.

QUERY STRINGS

In addition to the standard Internet address format, sites sometimes append their URL to provide additional information that only has meaning for that website. This is much like the "attn:" portion of a mailing address—it calls attention to the recipient of the letter, but does not have much meaning to anyone else reading or routing the mail to its destination. It provides additional information for the website to respond to, once the request has been properly routed to the apartment (subdomain) within the building (the domain).

This additional data is usually referred to as a "query string," primarily because it is used heavily in search engines to provide search criteria. Now why should you care about query strings, and why would I bring it up in a book on cyber safety? Because understanding query strings can help you determine how your computer is being used and what the people using your computer are actively searching for. By understanding a query string, you can determine whether someone inadvertently came across some illicit content or if that person intentionally tried to locate that content.

While some websites make an attempt to render this data unreadable to the human eye by encrypting the data into a large number or set of meaningless characters, most just use standard text formatting, which permits easy interpretation. When you understand how to read this, you can understand exactly what someone has been doing on your computer; these query strings act like a trail of breadcrumbs.

A typical query string looks like this:

> http://www.google.com/search?hl=en&q=george+washington&btnG=Google+Search

By ignoring the extraneous data encoded in this query string, one can see that someone used this computer to search for George Washington data on Google. The following version of this URL highlights the sections that provide this information.

> http://**www**.google.com/**search**?hl=en&q=**george+washington**&btnG=Google+Search

The "www" tells us that they used the standard Google.com subdomain, which allows searching of textual data. In the query string, we see the words "George" and "Washington," indicating what they searched for. The rest of the characters on this query string are only meaningful to the search engine and can be ignored for our purposes.

In this next example, we see that the search was slightly modified, allowing us to search for images of George Washington, rather than textual references to George Washington:

> http://**images**.google.com/images?hl=en&q=george+washington&um=1&ie=UTF-8&sa=N&tab=wi

Here are a couple of URLs showing the same searches on different search engines. See if you can pick out the relevant data to understand what search engine was used, what type of data was being searched for (text or images), and what keywords were used in the search:

> http://search.yahoo.com/search?p=george+washington&fr=yfp-t-501-s&toggle=1&cop=mss&ei=UTF-8

> http://images.search.yahoo.com/search/images?p=george+washington&fr=yfp-t-501&toggle=1&cop=mss&ei=UTF-8

> http://www.ask.com/web&q=george+washington&search=search&qsrc=0&o=0&1=dir

http://www.ask.com/pictures?q=george+washington&search=search&qsrc=178&o=0&1=dir

http://www.bing.com/search?q=george+washington&FORM=BFWD

http://www.bing.com/images/search?q=george+washington&FORM=BIFD

Understanding how to interpret a query string gives you a powerful tool to help you determine if someone just happened to stumble across some inappropriate data or if he was actively searching for it. This data is kept in your browser history. It is also tracked and recorded by many of the filters available today. Law enforcement uses this same method to gather evidence to prove that someone performed searches for specific data.

For example, the following is an email notification from a filter program. It indicates the URL that was attempted along with some information about what might be found at that location. Notice how our new understanding of URLs and query strings provides additional insight into what the individual was attempting to do.

Date: Sunday, March 23, 2008
Time: 03:13 PM
User Name: Jimbo
Computer Name: MUSIC_ROOM

Action: Block!
Attempted Site: www.youtube.com/results?search_query=alvin+and+the+chipmunks+-face+down&search_type=

Categorized As: Adult/Mature

****
*** This is an automated email. Do not reply. ***
****

We can see that this block was simply due to an innocent search for a video of Alvin and the Chipmunks, rather than something more insiduous.

Understanding how to decode an Internet address, as well as a query string, provides you with important information regarding the use of your computer. In Chapter 7 we will discuss filters and monitoring applications in more detail. Most of them will allow you to receive email notifications of actions taken on your computers, like the one above. Many of these applications also provide reporting tools that will show you the URLs, the actions taken, and who was logged into the computer when the activity occurred. All of this is important information when attempting to figure out how your computer has been used.

SECURE SITES

Let us take a short sidebar and talk about secure sites. This is important for two reasons: 1. secure sites are one mechanism that people use to bypass filters and purveyors of pornography know this, and 2. criminals take advantage of our misunderstanding of secure sites to more easily steal our information, which can lead to identity theft.

Most of us are familiar with the following lock image which appears in the browser address bar, indicating that you are connected to a secure site:

Figure 2: The Lock from Internet Explorer

Be aware, however, that this icon indicates only that the site is using the secure version of the Internet protocol to transmit a website's data to and from your computer. In addition to the lock icon, another way you can determine that you have a secure connection to a website is "https" in the URL. If the Internet address starts with "https:" instead of the more common "http:," the site is using a secure connection.

Using a secure connection is much like sending a registered letter. It uses the Hyper-Text Transmission Protocol, but adds a critical element which ensures that only the intended recipient will receive the data. Just like you could find out who received a registered letter by looking at the signature provided when the letter was delivered, you can be certain that data sent across an HTTPS communication is viewable only by the computer sending the data and the computer that receives the data. That is, the content that is shared between the server and your browser is encrypted and cannot be viewed or modified by someone while in transit. As we will see later, this also means that it cannot be viewed by most filters (see Chapter 7).

Although a secure connection ensures that all communication between your browser and the target site is secure, it does not ensure that you are connected to the website you think you are. As we learned above, the domain is the primary indicator of who you are dealing with. People use tricky methods to imitate or spoof a reputable or familiar organization, only to then steal your information or provide you with an experience that you were not anticipating. For example, let's say your bank is Joe's Bank, and you do your online banking at www.joesbank.com. You are familiar with this name and trust entering your personal data there. One day you receive an email, apparently from joesbank.com, asking you to click on a link and re-enter your personal data. When you click on the link, your browser opens and you are taken to joesbank.myplace.com or maybe to www.joesbank.myplace.com, or even possibly to www.myplace.com/joesbank. Note that none of these URLs are actually Joe's Bank. Despite the fact that these sites' URLs contain variations of "joesbank" in the address, and that they may look exactly like Joe's Bank, complete with the appropriate logos and images that you are used to seeing when you do business online with Joe's Bank; they are, instead, a completely different location. Indeed, you have been tricked into walking into the wrong building!

To further complete the charade, the spoofers will often secure their site so you see the lock at the bottom of the screen. It is important to remember that all the lock icon tells you is that the current website has established a secure connection. In others words, the phishers have established a secure connection to your browser, thereby ensuring that only they can steal your data! Once you enter your personal information, you have fallen into their trap and provided them with the information they need to steal your money or your identity.

As an example, here is a message that this author received while writing this book:

My first clue that something is not right is that I am not a member of this particular Credit Union (which I have obscured here, since it is merely a victim too). If I were a member, this email message might lure me to click on the link and enter the requested information. However, on closer examination, the "Click here" link actually takes me to the following URL, which is clearly displayed in the address box of the browser:

https://static-71-189-199-217.lsanca.dsl-w.badplace.net/home/index.html[8]

Using our knowledge of Internet addresses, it is easy to see that this is not actually the credit union in question, but rather some location on badplace.net. In this case, the criminals have not even attempted to hide their real address. They simply assume that you will not look closely enough at the URL to determine that it is a fake. The page that appears in the browser actually looks just like the real credit union page, complete with logos, trademarks, and other identifying images and text. If I were a member of this credit union, this page would look very familiar to me. And since the phishers used the secure transport (HTTPS), the lock appears in my browser, giving me one more visual cue that I am at the real credit union's website, when, in fact, I am not.

After a close inspection of the URL, it is clear to see that some unscrupulous individuals have rented space on badplace.net and have created a page that is intended to look like the credit union page. They are trying to entice me to enter my personal banking information, which they can then use to clean out my account.

Using our newfound understanding of web addresses, we are now armed to defend ourselves against such blatant attempts to obtain our personal information.

WHAT TO DO

> In this chapter we learned how to decode Internet addresses so you can now use this information to read the reports and Internet usage history provided by your Internet browser, filters, or monitoring software. By understanding how to decode an Internet address, you can immediately determine whether your computer has been used to visit inappropriate sites. To really understand these addresses, spend some time surfing the Internet, watch the address change as you visit different sites, make search requests, and perform other operations. Just like learning a second language, the more you practice, the better you will understand how it all works. And just like a second language, you will always be able to understand more than you can speak. Luckily, in the virtual world of the Internet, you don't have to "speak" the language—all you need to know is how to read it.

> We also talked about secure sites. Don't be fooled by the tricks malicious individuals use to try to steal your data. Be especially careful when dealing with financial and credit card sites. Don't ever follow links sent to you via email, even if they look valid. Sometimes the change is very small, and would be very difficult to notice. Just two transposed characters, or a different TLD, will take you to a completely different website. Always type the URL directly into your browser yourself, or use your favorites to return to your online financial institutions. If you are ever in doubt about whether a message came from your financial institution, call them before you act on the request. As the old

saying goes, an ounce of prevention is worth a pound of cure.

Notes

1. Gordon B. Hinckley, "Fear Not, Only Believe," *New Era*, Jan. 2000.

2. From a strictly technical perspective, this is not completely true. There are "intranets," which are mini-internets where the address is only valid for that particular network of computers. These are found inside of companies, within homes, or in any other location where a group of computers wants to communicate but doesn't want to make that data available to the entire world. In that case, the URL needs to be unique only within that particular set of computers.

3. There are some exceptions to this; some URLs will tack on a "country code" at the end. This concept is covered later in the book.

4. Usually, this is just an IP address, consisting of four sets of numbers separated by periods. However, it is possible to have a domain name associated with your home computer as well, if your Internet Service Provider allows this capability and if you have request it from them.

5. Note that each of these acronyms ends in "P," which stands for protocol (HTTP, FTP, POP, SMTP, FTP). Protocols are the mechanism upon which the Internet is built. Unfortunately, new protocols are constantly being created as new ways are needed to send content across the Internet. Keeping up with new protocols is one of the problems associated with any technology that attempts to protect you from the dangers of the Internet.

6. Technically speaking, this occurs in the opposite direction on the Internet. That is, you request content *from* an Internet address and that content is returned to your browser.

7. As we will see in Chapter 7, this is actually one method for getting around filters. If the filter is set to look at a URL, then entering the IP address instead will bypass the filter completely.

8. Note that I also changed the domain here to "badplace." This is another attempt to protect the innocent domain provider from being associated with the unscrupulous acts of those who rent space on its servers.

7
FILTERING THE INTERNET

"Guard your homes. How foolish it seems to install bars and bolts and electronic devices against thieves and molesters while more insidious intruders stealthily enter and despoil."[1]

Gordon B. Hinckley

How Filters Work

A filter can be thought of as a guard that you hire to protect your home from unwanted content. Just as a real guard would stand at the physical entrance to your house and stop certain people from coming in, so a filter stands at the digital entrance to your home and prevents certain content from coming in. If you hired a physical guard, you could have him look at every piece of mail that arrives at your address, then decide whether the content was something that you wanted in your home or not. If it was, then the guard would put the letter through the mail slot and it would be successfully delivered into your home. If the guard identified the letter as content that you did not want in your home, he would set it aside and not allow it to be placed in the mail slot in your front door—that is, the content would not be

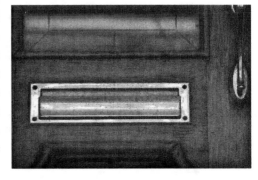

allowed into your home. A filter works in exactly this way.

There are essentially two things that a filter can use to determine whether to allow content or not: it can look at the URL (i.e., the return address of the letter), or it can inspect the content (i.e., the letter itself). Following our analogy, the first option would be similar to the security guard simply reviewing the return address of every letter; the second option would be like having the guard actually open every letter and read it, prior to passing it through the mail slot. Since both options have their limitations, most filters today use both methods to completely inspect data prior to allowing it onto your computer.

Let's take a moment and discuss these two methods in more detail.

URL Lists

Filtering content using a URL list, or the return address of the letter, is much like blocking a channel on your TV or requesting that your phone number be placed on a specific company's "do not call" list. In essence, you inform your filter that you do not want any content from designated URLs to be allowed onto your computer, regardless of what the content is. Some of the content may not be offensive, but you want it blocked nonetheless. In this case, your filter (or the guard standing at your front door) does not look at the content at all. It only looks at the return address. This is a wide-net approach. Consider what would happen if you blocked your local online newspaper website; not only would you block the news content, but also the classified ads, the sports section, the letters to the editor, and so forth.

When using a URL list, by definition the only thing the filter has access to is the URL itself. There are two ways, then, for a URL, or list-based, filter to operate: white list mode or black list mode. These options are described below:

➤ White List Mode

White list mode allows content only from designated URLs. In other words, everything is blocked unless you specifically grant access to it.

This is a very conservative and restrictive approach to the Internet. It assumes that all content is undesirable until proven otherwise. You are responsible for entering all addresses you want people to access from your computer. If someone attempts to access a site that is not on your list, it is blocked. This is usually used when parents only want their children to go to a handful of websites, and block everything else.

One of the problems with this approach is that more and more websites are linking to content from other websites. The filter has no way to determine the difference between something typed into the browser and a link on a page, so it will block all access to anything that is not on the whitelist. This causes some websites to not function correctly.

> Black List Mode

Black list mode blocks content only from designated URLs. In other words, everything is allowed unless you specifically deny access to it.

This is a more liberal approach to the Internet. It assumes that all content is okay until it is proven undesirable. You are responsible for entering all addresses you want to block, which means that you need to list every site that has inappropriate content. Since this is an overwhelming task, and because new websites appear all the time, most filter companies maintain a black list for you. This means, however, that your computer must have access to the newest list and frequently update itself to stay in sync with the latest Internet content.

One of the major problems with this approach is that bad content is appearing on new websites daily, and in order to block them you need to either trust that your filter company is somehow staying on top of it, or you need to find these sites and block them yourself. Neither are very desirable options.

As you can see, neither of these options are very efficient and both require a significant amount of maintenance. Given the dynamic nature of the Internet, it is almost impossible for either a black list or a white list to remain completely valid over time. The filters will either over- or under-block Internet content. Therefore, it is necessary to supplement URL lists with some type of content inspection. There are not many commercial filters today that still rely solely on a URL list.

CONTENT ANALYSIS

Inspecting content is like using your TV parental controls to block content from any channel based on the content's rating (rather than just always blocking a certain channel). The main difference between a computer filter and your TV controls, though, is that on the computer, the filter attempts to rate the content as you access it in real time, while the content on television comes pre-rated according to a standardized rating system. Television filtering is a much easier problem because the parental control uses the standard rating system to enforce your choices for your family. The ratings are pre-determined and well communicated, and they are broadcast to your home along with the television show itself. (We will discuss television ratings in more detail in Chapter 12.) Internet content is not as regulated, and thus the computer filter has to use sophisticated linguistic algorithms to determine what the content is as you surf the Internet. Consequently, it is a much less accurate and less reliable process.

Even though it is not perfect, content analysis is an important aspect of most commercial filters today. Content analysis searches for certain words or sequences of words on an page and will block content that appears to be inappropriate. These sophisticated algorithms are actually quite accurate and provide a much-needed layer of protection that is critical to filtering content into our homes. Using Content Analysis is like asking our guard to open each letter, read through it, and determine if the content is something we should allow into our home. While not completely accurate, it is much more rigorous than a URL list.

FILTER TYPES

Apart from the two filtering techniques, there are also different places to install the filter. Think of this like the different places the guard can stand to protect your home. The guard can be on your front porch, in the street in front of your property, or even at the post office to intercept your mail before it is even loaded on the mail truck. Similarly, some filters are installed on your computer, some are installed at the gateway to your home, and some operate out in the Internet before traffic is routed to your home. We will review each type of filter in the following sections, along with the strengths and weaknesses of each one so you can determine which filter is best for your family's needs.

Software Filters

A software filter is an application that is installed on your computer for the purpose of filtering Internet content. This may also be known as a "client-side" filter. The term "client-side" comes from the concept of a "client-server" application, in which a portion of the application resides on a machine that is used by a person, (referred to as the client) and the other portion of the application resides on a machine whose only job is to "serve" data to the clients (referred to as the server). These two computers communicate with each other, sending data back and forth to accomplish the overall task of the client-server software.

Software filters are applications that you download from the Internet or purchase in a store, then install on your computer. The filter interjects itself into the communication chain between the browser on your computer and the Internet so that the filter can watch the communication and perform its guard duty. Software filters are usually the most robust, and offer the greatest level of protection and flexibility—not only from pornography, but from other dangers as well (such as online predators, online gaming, and so forth).

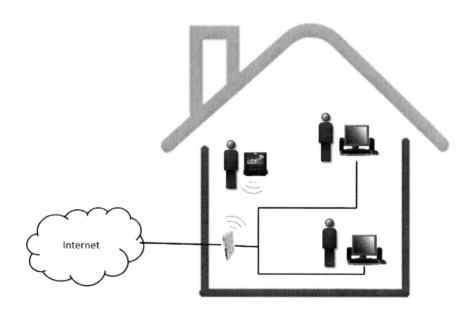

In our analogy, this option is like putting a guard at your front door. A software filter looks at data on your computer, so it will either inspect the URL before the request gets routed off of your computer (the guard will look at your mail before dropping it into the outgoing mail box), or it will inspect the content as it arrives on your computer (the guard will inspect all incoming mail). It is important to note that because the guard is actually on your property, bad mail will also make it onto your property, but the guard stops it before it gets to you. Similarly, in the virtual world, the bad content will arrive on your computer, but the filter intercepts it before it displays on the screen. This is an important distinction because it means that it is possible that some inappropriate images could end up on your computer that were never actually viewed by anyone using your computer. The images arrived on the computer, but the filter did not allow them to be displayed.

Hardware Filters

Hardware filters are also sometimes called "gateway" filters. In a home network, the gateway is the single entry-point for the Internet in your home. For high-speed access, this may be a cable modem or a DSL

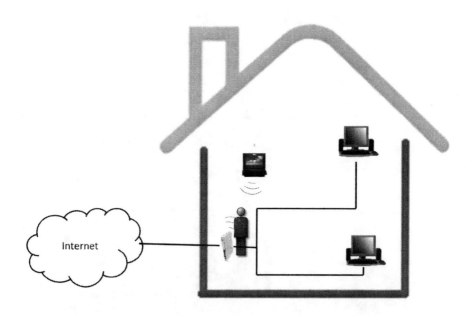

router—it all depends on how your computers access the Internet. Some of these routers, or modems, have built-in software that filters the Internet. This is an example of a *hardware filter* or *gateway filter*. You do not need to install anything on your computer; the mere fact that your computer uses this gateway to access the Internet ensures that the content is filtered.

This option is similar to the guard standing at your mailbox, intercepting the mail directly from the mailman before it is placed in your mailbox. The bad content is intercepted before it ever arrives on your computer. Regardless of what protocol is used, all inbound or outbound data must pass through this gateway. We will learn more about why this is important later in this chapter when we discuss limited protocol support.

Internet or Proxy Filtering

Some Internet Service Providers (ISPs) will offer filtering as part of their service. If they don't, you could sign up with a service on the Internet, called a *proxy*, that will filter your content on the Internet before sending it to your home. Since this works on the Internet, there is nothing to install on your computer. And if this service is offered by your ISP, then there is usually nothing to configure—you simply turn this service on with your

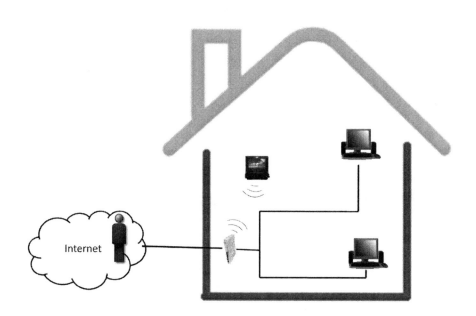

ISP, and it filters all content. If you are using a proxy service, then you must configure your individual computer to use the proxy filter. That doesn't necessarily mean you'll need to install anything on your computer, but you will need to ensure that the computer is configured to use that proxy. Like hardware filters, internet or proxy filters are usually simplistic and do not have the robust features of a software filter.

Continuing our analogy of a guard watching our mail, this would be comparable to having our guard stand at the post office and inspect each piece of mail before it is loaded onto the mail truck for delivery.

Filters and Search Engines

Search engines have become extremely popular, and quite often seem to be our on-ramp to the Internet. The immense content available on the Internet is categorized and presented to us from these search engines, making it easy to access. Of course, search engines do not usually filter their content, so they can also provide easy access to extremely inappropriate material.

Some filters allow you to prevent searches on certain terms, but usually they require you to enter those terms yourself. This requires that you think of every possible offensive or inappropriate search term . . . which is close to impossible since most of us don't even know all the current jargon. Obviously, this is not ideal.

As we learned in Chapter 1, even innocuous searches can often present us with some very inappropriate content, which is what our children have discovered while researching their homework assignments. Pornographers know how critical searching is to our Internet usage, so they do everything they can to ensure that their content appears when we search for anything. Consequently, an image search on just about any topic, no matter how innocuous, will usually yield some pornographic images.

Many search engines have a "safe search" feature. This feature is widely misunderstood, and again, provides a false sense of security. You enable the safe search capability by simply finding the options page for your search engine, then selecting the safe search option.[2]

There are several problems with "safe search." Here are just a few:

➢ It is just as easy to turn off safe search as it is to turn it on. There is no real way to prohibit others from turning this feature off to perform a search, then turning it back on when they are done.

Some filters have added the ability to force safe search to remain on, which is a great feature, but it relies on the assumption that the search engine will always enforce its safe search in the same way. If the search engine changes the way it handles safe search, then this filter feature breaks, and you are no longer guaranteed forced safe searches.

➢ The search engine companies are not in the business of filtering. They have provided the safe search capability to ease the concern of parents, but it is not their primary goal to limit search results for those who come to their site. This is in direct opposition to their desired goal, which is to provide as much data as possible on the subject which is being searched. This is not to say that these companies are not being honest in their attempts to protect our children—but it is clear that limiting searches is in direct opposition to their business model.

➢ Most of the safe search technologies are currently based on textual analysis of the search criteria, with some additional algorithmic analysis of the content returned from the search. Pornographers understand this, so to circumvent the safe search feature, they simply provide innocuous content to describe their pornographic images. Images are not filtered by the safe search and the associated text doesn't trip any warning signs, so the safe search allows the search result to be returned. It is not until someone sees this result and brings it to the attention of the search engine company that it will be removed from the safe search results.

➢ Not all search sites implement a safe search functionality. If you have a filter that forces safe searches, it can only do so for those search engines that support it. If your children want to find a site that does not enforce safe searches, it is relatively easy to do so. And remember, image searches performed without safe search turned on will quite often return some pornographic images.

The lesson here is that safe search is not an infallible solution to the pornography problem on the Internet. Do not be lulled into a false sense of security simply because you have turned on safe search or have a filter that forces safe search to be turned on.

FILTERS AND USER-GENERATED CONTENT

In the past few years a new word has entered the English language: *blog*. This comes from "Web Log" which encompasses many concepts ranging from an online journal to self-published articles on any number of topics. According to Paul Ottelini, President of Intel Corporation, there are over 100,000 blog entries created every day.[3] Like the proliferation of reality TV shows that appeared after the success of *Survivor*, user-generated content sites are quickly becoming the preferred mechanism for sharing data on the Internet.

User-generated content sites refer to those sites that allow individuals to place whatever they like on the Internet, sometimes located on a web address that is well-known (like YouTube or MySpace), and other times located at a specific URL known only to some people (like personal blogs). These sites act as a digital parking lot for the general public. They allow anyone to create and upload content to their site for others to view. This content does not go through any type of standard rating system, and the linguistic algorithms that filters use are relatively useless against uploaded video or images. This means that unless you block the entire site by adding the URL to your block list (which means you have to know about the site to begin with), the site is mainly unfiltered if it is primarily image and video content—such as YouTube. If enough people type comments onto the page that describe what the video relates to, then the linguistic algorithms have something to work from and they can categorize it—but this is only based on the textual comments added to the site. This is a very unreliable method of categorizing the video content.

There are two main reasons why we should be very concerned about user-generated image and video content sites when we have a filter installed.

1. There is a false sense of security with filters. I cannot tell you how many times I have had to explain this to parents. Their usual response is, "But I have a filter installed—won't that block the inappropriate content from YouTube?" Too often we install a filter and then feel that our job of protecting our children online is done. Unfortunately, filters are only a piece of the puzzle. We still need to remain very aware of what our children are doing online and how they spend their time. If they are spending large amounts of time on sites like YouTube, we need to know what they are seeing and why. The best way to do this is the old-fashioned

way: communication and direct questions; but more about this in Chapter 13.

2. Undesirable content is easily masked to appear innocuous. It is a sad fact of our life today that people want to push their inappropriate content into our homes. In the early days of the Internet, people would register domain names that were a common misspelling of a popular site and would post pornographic content there. This made it very easy for someone to stumble across a bad site. We learned about an example of this earlier: whitehouse.com (instead of whitehouse.gov) used to host pornography, until a law was passed that made this type of deception illegal. Unfortunately, there are no similar laws for user-generated content (yet). So, someone could easily film inappropriate content, label it "Sponge Bob," and upload it for our children to find.

The bottom line here is that we need to be very careful about what our children are viewing online. We cannot allow ourselves to be lulled into a false sense of security just because we have a filter. User-generated content sites are growing in popularity and only some of them are regulated in any way.

TIME CONTROLS IN FILTERS

Most filters today also have time controls, which allow parents to set some boundaries regarding the amount of time children can spend on the Internet. In years past, children's activities were controlled by natural bounds. My parents didn't need to tell me when to stop playing sports. The environment or the activity itself naturally limited our play—whether it was the setting of the sun, the park closing, enough of my friends going home that there were simply not enough of us left to enjoy a game, or just being too tired to run around any more. In the end, we always had to wrap up our activities and plan to meet again the next day. It was the natural order of things.

Digital activities today do not have these natural boundaries. Online games generate the adrenaline rush that helps keep us awake; moreover, our bodies don't get physically tired from typing on the keyboard or moving the mouse. Therefore, we can spend all night in a virtual world and not even notice the time flying by. When friends drop off, we can continue playing with the myriad of other people who remain online, or we can just play against the computer-generated characters by ourselves. Chatting online with friends can continue well into the night, long after the natural bounds of the physical world would have forced us to disband and return to our homes.

Making use of the time controls feature in a filter allows parents to help enforce their own time restrictions on computer activities. When the time runs out, the filter will simply "unplug" the Internet.[4]

LIMITATIONS OF FILTERS

One of my major concerns when writing this book was that I did not want it to be a how-to reference book people could use to find the very content that we are trying to protect our families from. However, I balanced this danger against the benefit of educating parents about how people who want to find this content do so. As I have mentioned several times already, one of the unfortunate side-effects of installing a filter is the false sense of security that it provides. Most teenagers can get around just about any filter if they really want to, and parents need to know how this is done so they can watch for the warning signs.

The methods that I will share here are all freely available on the Internet, and anyone who wants to bypass a filter can easily obtain this information for himself. While there is some danger that this book may be used to bypass protections that have been placed on the computer, it is far more important for us to be educated about the methods people use so we can protect against them. With that caveat, here are some of the major methods that people use to get past filters.

LIMITED PROTOCOL SUPPORT

As we discussed in Chapter 6, each protocol can be considered a different delivery mechanism, just like different delivery methods can bring packages to your home. We have talked about the similarities between a filter and a security guard standing at your front door. In the world of the Internet, this guard can only look at the protocols, or delivery mechanisms, that it is aware of. Most filters watch the HTTP protocol, since this is the primary delivery mechanism for content via a web browser. There are many other protocols, however, that deliver content into your home which the guard cannot look at. Secure HTTP, or HTTPS, is one such protocol. This is similar to a wax seal put on a letter that does not allow the letter to be opened prior to its delivery to the intended recipient. The security guard cannot open the letter to inspect the contents without breaking the seal. Only the more sophisticated filters today can filter secure content—most simply ignore all secure content and allow it through.

There are also other protocols that can deliver the package directly into your home. Some great examples are peer-to-peer applications, file-sharing, file transfer, and email protocols. If the security guard can only look at U.S. mail, then the FedEx, or UPS delivery person will walk right past. Similarly, these alternative protocols may simply bypass your filter. It is important that you understand which protocols your filter recognizes and which protocols your children use. If your filter cannot screen these protocols, it may allow you to simply turn them off, so they cannot deliver any content to your home at all. In essence, the security guard simply stops all deliveries except for those which he can inspect. A great example would be peer-to-peer applications, which operate on their own protocols, and which are designed to deliver content into your home without allowing inspection by any filter. We will discuss these types of applications in more detail in Chapter 9.

ANONYMOUS SURFING

One of the most popular methods of bypassing filters is by using so-called anonomizers, or anonymous surfing sites. These are sites that are designed by the website creator to have a hidden URL. This is usually done by making the anonymous surfing site a proxy for the actual site, or in other words they create a browser within a browser. The web browser on

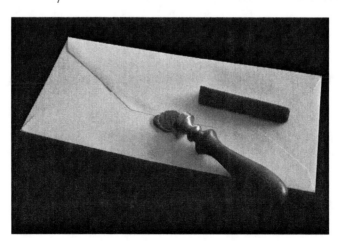

the client machine never gets the actual website address; rather, all it sees is a string of characters that has meaning only to the proxy site. As far as the browser on your computer—and any associated filter—knows the content is simply coming from the proxy site. In reality, the browser within the browser is bringing all kinds of content into your home that the filter would normally reject.

In terms of our analogy, each letter that is delivered to our guard this way, has exactly the same return address, thus rendering the URL list ineffective. Unless the guard can open the letter and inspect the contents, the letter is allowed through the mail slot and into your home, since the return address appears to be innocuous. Of course, you could add the proxy site URL to your list, but the people behind these anonymous surfing proxy sites know this, and create new URLs almost daily, making it virtually impossible for a list-based filter to keep up.

This is not a new trick and many filters have started looking at the content as well as the address, so it does not matter whether the inappropriate content comes from an adult site or a proxy site—the filter can still catch it. To get around this, the creators of these anonymous surfing sites have now started hosting their proxy pages as secure site (https), thus creating another difficulty for filters. As we saw in Chapter 6, secure sites encrypt their content before they send it to the client, thus making it extremely difficult for our filter to scan the contents before it gets into our home. This would be like the proxy not only changing the return address, but also putting each letter into a manila envelope and sealing it so only we could open it after it arrived. The guard could not inspect the content, and the return address would always be allowed into our home.

By employing this method, the website owner not only hides the URL from the filter, but he also hides the content so he can effectively bypass most filters between the proxy site and the browser. Again, only the most sophisticated filters will successfully filter this content.

When these methods are employed, someone can easily browse any content he desires without tampering with the filter. There would be no evidence in the filter logs of someone turning off the filter, entering the override password, or doing anything else that would indicate that someone had been trying to view inappropriate content. The browser history, as well as the filter history, would only show the secure proxy site. This, in itself, should be an indication of concern—if you find secure proxy sites in your browser history, it is time to have a discussion with those using your computer. There are very few reasons to use secure proxy sites other than to try to hide your tracks or to bypass a filter.

These proxy sites are dedicated to trying to help people get around filters. Because so many of the early filters were based solely on the URL, the creators of these proxy sites had to get creative to continue to bypass the filter. To circumvent the problem of having their proxy URL blocked, the creators of these sites began creating new URLs almost daily, as mentioned earlier, making it extremely difficult for the filters to keep up with them.

They would then create an index site that listed all their proxy URLs, so one could visit the index site and select a proxy URL that had not yet been added to the filter's black list.

Because of the way that these proxy sites hide their real URLs, they are especially effective against both gateway and client filters.

Bootable CDs

Another very popular method for bypassing filters is to simply bypass the operating system altogether. Linux is a very small operating system, which can be booted directly from a CD. All one has to do is insert the CD in the drive, ensure that the computer will boot from the CD, then restart the computer. The filter associated with the original operating system is now disabled, and the individual has immediate Internet access to any location he likes.

This method works for both client side and Internet or proxy filters. For a hardware filter, the connection to the Internet must still go through the gateway filter, regardless of what operating system is in use, so this is not an effective way to bypass a hardware filter. However, combining the bootable CD method with an open wireless access point would still be an effective way to bypass a gateway filter as this method leaves no history of sites visited in the operating system's log files.

Hijacking wireless access

When a gateway filter is in use, the user only needs to find a different path to the Internet to bypass the filter. For example, if any neighbor happens to have an unsecured wireless access point set up, this could provide a way for your computer to access the Internet without going through your gateway filter. One simply has to turn on wireless access, which is available in the more popular operating systems today, and search for an unsecured wireless connection. Unfortunately, many people set up wireless access in their homes and do not secure the connection, leaving it available for anyone to piggy-back on their connection. If your neighbors don't have a filter on their wireless connection, your computer could have direct access to anything on the Internet. Alternatively, there are many "hotspots" around town where people can take their laptop and connect to the Internet via the wireless hot spot. If you do not have a software filter on your laptop, this unsecured connection will allow it to browse anywhere it wants, completely unfiltered.

Browsers

Some client-side filters only work with certain browsers. You will need to understand which browsers are supported by your filter in order to know if this is a concern for you or not.

There are many free browsers available and they can be downloaded and installed in minutes. If your filter supports only Internet Explorer, then someone could easily download Firefox, Opera, Netscape or any other browser to have direct access to the Internet.

Web Accelerators

A web accelerator is a method of increasing the speed of sending data across the wire by compressing that data into a smaller size. Web accelerators are usually employed by users with a dial-up connection (that is, users who use their phone lines to connect to the Internet), but there is nothing to stop you from using a web accelerator with a high-speed data line as well. However, the only reason that someone would use a web accelerator with a high-speed connection would be to hide something, because web accelerators don't provide any benefits on a high-speed line other than that they bypass filters.

The web accelerator works in a very similar way to encryption. It usually involves a proxy server that compresses the data from every website that is visited, then sends the data to the client in its compressed form. The client must have software that can decompress the data and display it in the browser. This transaction acts much like a secure site in that neither the data nor the URL is available for the filter to inspect. Here again, this method allows the user to surf any sites he wants while leaving the filter installed and operational, and without tampering with the filter in any way.

Using a web accelerator to bypass filters is effective for both client-side and server-side filters.

IMAGE SEARCHES

Most of the popular filters are text-based, which means that they operate by employing sophisticated linguistic algorithms to analyze the text on any given web page. Consequently, filters do not handle images or videos very well. The filter can only attempt to categorize the image based on the URL or the text that appears on the page with the image or video. The search engine will gather the search results and display them all in the results page, housed by the search engine (that is, the URL will be "google.com," or "yahoo.com" or whatever search engine is being used). Pornographers know this, so they create pages with innocuous text to go along with extremely graphic images.

This problem is prolific when using image search sites, since these search engines scour the Internet and return images that appear to match the search criteria. The only way they can associate images with the search criteria is by referencing the text that accompanies the image. When a search engine returns the results in its own page (google.com, yahoo. com, and so forth), the filter sees only the search engine URL and the text returned with each hit. So, unless you block the search engine's URL, anyone using your computer can find extremely graphic images simply by performing an image search. It is only when the user attempts to click on the image itself that the filter might kick in and block the result. When you try to follow-up on these searches, the log files only show that the user visited the search site—it does not list the sites that made up the search engine's results.

Even if you are using a filter that analyzes the content, you are at risk. Remember that the content, as far as the filter is concerned, is just the text associated with the image. If the associated text doesn't reflect what is actually in the image, the filter allows it through. Bad people design their descriptions of these images to bypass filters and get inappropriate content into your home without your permission.

HOW TO CHOOSE THE RIGHT FILTER

Given the many options available for filtering in the home, people tend to get confused regarding how to select the right filter for their needs. There are some simple questions that you can ask yourself that will help you determine which filter will best fit your families' needs. They are:

1. What devices are you trying to protect?

Many devices today are Internet-enabled, and would benefit from protection. It is important to keep in mind that we are not just talking about desktop computers, but also any laptops, gaming consoles, set-top TVs, or any other Internet-enabled device in your home that uses your network to access the Internet. Remember that cell phones do not fall into this category, since they use the cell phone network for their Internet access. However, just about everything else that accesses the Internet in your home uses your home network to do so.

If you have several different devices that connect to the Internet, it is probable that you have a broadband connection. You might want to investigate the hardware solution first, since its possible that some of the devices in your home that have access to the internet cannot support filtering software. For example, many game consoles can access the Internet via a wireless connection in the home, but you cannot install any software on these devices. If you are able to use a hardware filter, then all the devices in your home will automatically be filtered simply by the fact that they connect to the Internet through your hardware device.

2. What operating systems (OSs) are run in your home?

An operating system is the application that you interact with to operate your computer. It is what "boots up" the computer and what you log in to for access to that computer (although not all operating systems require a login). The most common operating systems are the several versions of Windows from Microsoft Corp (Windows XP, Vista, and a few older versions), and a couple of versions for the Mac from Apple. There are a few other popular OSs, but they are not in wide enough use to be listed separately here.

As a very general rule of thumb, if you have multiple operating systems in your home, you probably want to consider a hardware filter. A hardware filter doesn't require direct interaction with the OS and you don't have to worry about whether it will operate in the same way on all of your computers. Having said that, there are a couple of software filters on the market today that support both Windows and Mac operating systems.[5] If you only have two or three computers to filter and you have a heterogeneous operating system environment, you may want to do just a little bit of research before deciding that a software filter is not for you. Remember that software filters tend to be more robust and protect you from more dangers than hardware and Internet or proxy filters.

In the latest shipping versions of operating systems for Windows and Mac, there are built-in filters that you can use for free as part of the system. They are not as robust as some of the commercial filters that you would purchase, but they are certainly better than no filter at all. Before you purchase a solution, check to see if you are running the latest version of the operating system, and whether the built-in filter will suit your needs.

Here are the major operating systems on the market today, and the software filtering options available for them:

Windows: Most of the filters that you can easily find on the Web today are made for the latest versions of Windows. Vista, which is the newest version from Microsoft, has some built-in filtering, which may be sufficient for many people's needs. It is primarily a list-based solution, however, so you will want to take that into consideration. (Recall our discussion earlier in this chapter about the difference between list-based and URL-based filters.)

Many of the current filters for purchase are compatible with Windows Vista filtering and integrate well with it. Vista filtering is designed so that the built-in functionality turns itself off if a new filter is installed. That way, you do not have an extra filter slowing down your Internet browsing experience.

Mac: The latest operating system for the Mac is called Leopard and it also comes with some built-in filtering. There are not very many commercial filters available for the Mac today; to the best of my knowledge, there are only two commercial filters that support both Windows and Mac systems. Since the Mac is gaining again in popularity, I would expect this number to increase relatively quickly.

Linux: There are some free filters available for Linux, but most of them are purely list-based and are not maintained by a company, so you are on your own with regard to updates. The Linux operating system is supported by the open-source community, as is most of its available software. This means that there is not a company behind it, but rather, a group of individuals who put in personal time to maintain the software. This is actually a fairly good model for most software, but can be worrisome when it comes to a filter.

3. Do you have laptop computers in your home?

If you have laptops in the home, it is highly likely that these laptops access the Internet when away from home as well. People can access wireless networks in school, in libraries, on buses, and in many other wireless hotspots around town. If you want to be sure that these laptops are protected when away from home as well as in your home, then you would want a software filter or an Internet or proxy filter. A hardware filter would only protect the laptops when they connect to the Internet through the hardware device in your home.

On the flip side of that coin, however, is that if you have laptops in the home, and you have wireless access for those laptops you then need to consider whether you want to protect the other laptops that may make use of your wireless connections. That is, when friends or family bring their laptops into your home and use your wireless connection to surf the Internet, do you want them to be protected as well? If so, you would need to install a hardware filter so that anyone who connects to your wireless access would be protected as they access the Internet.

4. Do you want to prevent inadvertent access, or are you trying to stop someone from their deliberate attempts to view inappropriate material?

First, a word of warning. As we learned earlier in this chapter, all filtering technology has its weaknesses, and stopping someone who is intent on accessing inappropriate material is next to impossible. However, there are still some valid issues to consider when deciding what type of filter to purchase.

If you are trying to prevent inadvertent access, then any filter will do. If, however, you are trying to prevent someone from deliberately de-activating the filter to seek out inappropriate content, then you want to look at the more sophisticated commercial software filters. Generally speaking, hardware filters are harder to get around than software filters, but most of the commercial software filters on the market today are built so that you have to have quite a bit of technical expertise in order to subvert them. The free software-based filters tend to be easier to subvert.

As we learned earlier in this chapter, the most effective mechanism to bypass a software filter is to boot the computer from a Linux bootable

CD/DVD. If you are concerned about this, then you should consider a hardware filter. The reason for this is that a hardware filter doesn't care which operating system is trying to access the Internet—it simply filters all content that flows through the connection.

The most effective method to bypass a hardware filter is to find and use a secure proxy. The hardware filter can't decrypt the content, and thus can't filter it before it arrives on the computer. If you are concerned about this, then you should consider a commercial software filter with dynamic content filtering (rather than URL lists).

If you are truly concerned that someone is trying to bypass your protections, you may want to take a "belt and suspenders" approach, and install *both* a client-side (software) filter and a gateway (hardware) filter. There is no harm in doing so, as there is really no interaction between the two. It just means that you are doubly protected, and the bypass methodologies become more complicated and more technically challenging.

5. How do you connect to the Internet?

If you use a dial-up connection to the Internet, then you typically would not have a gateway in your home, so a hardware solution would not be appropriate for your environment. Instead, you should look for a software filter or an Internet or proxy filter.

6. Are you only concerned with access to pornography, or other dangerous activities, such as Internet predators, chat rooms, and so forth?

Generally speaking, both hardware and Internet or proxy filters are more rudimentary, and with a few exceptions will focus primarily on preventing access to pornography or other inappropriate content. They will not necessarily log chat sessions, provide usage reports based on each individual in the home, or any of the other more sophisticated filtering technologies that a commercial software filter would provide. If you are interested in this level of detailed reports, or in the other social-networking, chat room, or instant messaging features, you should consider a software filter.

7. Do you need to restrict the times that the Internet is used?

Some filters have time controls built into them so that you can turn off access to the Internet during certain times. If you do not want anyone to access the Internet from midnight to 6 am, for example, most software filters would have the ability to enforce this, whereas most hardware filters would not. Those hardware filters that do allow this would normally be an all-or-nothing solution: in other words, a software filter might let you allow some people to access the Internet at certain times while restricting others. With a hardware filter, every user has the same time restrictions.

8. How do you want to handle over-blocking?

Given the current state of filtering technology, you can rest assured that there will be times when you are blocked unnecessarily. That is, there will be times when you attempt to access a site that the filter thinks should be blocked, but you know the site to be okay. This is called over-blocking. With software filters, this is usually easy to handle; you can simply enter an administrator password and continue on to the site. With hardware and Internet or proxy filters, many times you need to contact the administrator of the filter (like your ISP, for example) and ask them to unblock the site. This usually takes time and can be a source of frustration.

WHERE TO GET MORE INFORMATION

Once you have the answers to these questions, you can then start deciding which specific filter is right for you. If you are interested in a hardware filter, it is probably best to go talk to someone in a computer store, or talk to your Internet service provider to see what they offer. It may be the case that the hardware device you already have has a filter capability and you simply need to turn it on.

If you are interested in a software filter, then you need to decide whether you want to purchase a commercial filter, which would have more features, or whether you want to find a free solution that will simply protect access to inappropriate content.

Commercial filters are currently available for around $40–$60 per computer per year. If you are interested in a commercial filter, take a look at http://www.internet-filter-review.com for a list of commercial filter programs and their feature comparisons in a side-by-side view. As of the writing of this book, the current software filters that I suggest people look at are: NetNanny by ContentWatch, SafeEyes by InternetSafety.com, and OnlineFamily.Norton by Symantec.

If you would like to try a more basic, free version of the software, first look at your operating system. As mentioned above, both of the latest versions of Windows and Mac operating systems have built-in software filters that may serve your needs. There are also free filters available for download that you can find online. Simply search for "free internet filter" to begin your research. One of the best free filters on the market as of the writing of this book is called K9, made by BlueCoat. You can find it with a simple search for "free Internet filter."

Notes

1. Gordon B. Hinckley, "Overpowering the Goliaths in Our Lives," *Ensign*, Jan. 2002, 2.
2. Since websites change frequently, it would not be very useful for me to provide exact steps for any given search engine here, but these options are usually not too difficult to find when you start looking for them.
3. Paul Ottelini, keynote speaker, Utah Technology Council Hall of Fame address, 2007.
4. In reality, this is a virtual pulling of the plug. Technically speaking, the filter will either stop all protocol activity or turn off the port through which that protocol communicates to the Internet.
5. Technically, "Mac" is not an operating system, but it is often referred to as such. For simplicity and ease of understanding, and to refrain from too much "tech speak," I take that liberty here as well.

8
SOCIAL NETWORKING

"Social networks on the Web can be used to expand healthy friendships as easily as they can be used by predators trying to trap the unwary. . . . Make sure that the choices you make in the use of new media are choices that expand your mind, increase your opportunities, and feed your soul."[1]

M. Russell Ballard

A New, Virtual Hang Out

The Internet has changed how young people meet, communicate and interact. Consider the story of Patrick Moberg, a twenty-one-year-old young man living in New York in 2007.[2] As he was riding the subway one day, he noticed the "girl of his dreams," and began that familiar debate in his head trying to convince himself that he should approach her and strike up a conversation. By the time he worked up the courage to do so, he saw her exit the subway car, and disappear into the sea of people on the platform. Wondering if he had missed the opportunity to meet his one soul mate, Patrick finally decided to use the Internet to find this amazing woman, so he created www.NYGirlOfMyDreams.com. He drew a picture of her, described in great detail what she was wearing (blue gym shorts), how she wore her hair (fancy, braided hair with a flower on the left) and what she was doing (writing in a journal on the train) in hopes of tracking her down. He sent the link to all of his friends and asked that they pass it on to everyone they knew, with the hope that it would somehow find her and she would respond. Within days, he was put in touch with Camille

Hayton, who was the very girl he shared a short subway ride with. They arranged a time to meet and have their first date. Patrick updated his website with a new cartoon drawing that simply said "found her." Welcome to the convergence of our physical world with the virtual one—social networking.

Social networking is becoming very popular on the Internet. We now have websites that are dedicated to allowing people to keep in touch, meet new people, and just generally network with other real people. These sites are called social networks, and they are places on the Internet where like-minded people go to converse, share pictures, talk about what is going on in their lives, and just virtually hang out. Popular social networking sites include MySpace.com, LinkedIn.com, and Twitter.com. The activities that one can participate in on a social networking site range from short updates regarding what someone is doing right now to online chats, picture and video sharing, and even online resumes, workshops, and job hunting.

The growth of social networks has been amazing to watch. In January 2009 Jeremiah Owyang, an analyst assigned to cover the social networking phenomenon, reported that social networks and blogs are now the fourth most popular online activity ahead of personal email. In that same report, he related the following statistics:[3]

Facebook

- 150 million people around the world are now actively using Facebook and almost half of them are using Facebook every day.
- Facebook has 54.5 million monthly unique visitors with a growth rate in the United States that averaged 3.8 percent per month more than last year.
- 175 million users are registered on the site, with 600,000 daily growth of users. Its fastest growing segment: "45 percent of Facebook's U.S. audience is now 26 years old or older."

MySpace

- 76 million members in MySpace U.S., with a U.S. growth rate of 0.8 percent per month.
- The average MySpace user now spends 4.4 hours on the site every month—a 5 percent increase over last month and a 31 percent increase year over year.

LinkedIn

+ 36 million members.
+ Adding new members at a rate of about one member per second.
+ It's gone from about 3.6 million unique monthly visitors a year ago to 7.7 million today.

DANGERS OF SOCIAL NETWORKING

Social networking sites are a great way to stay in touch with friends, but we need to ensure that we know how to make use of these sites safely, and be aware of what the possible dangers are. As these sites grow in popularity, they also attract predators. In early 2009, there was a story in the local Utah news[4] about a man who arranged a meeting with a woman he had met online. When he arrived at her apartment for the date, he was met by three men armed with a knife and a taser, who threatened him and took his wallet. They then drove him to a nearby ATM and told him to make a withdrawal. Luckily, the man was able to escape, and at least one of the suspects was arrested. Unfortunately, this story is not unique—many people meet online, and end up realizing when it is too late that they person they thought they had gotten to know online is in reality not the person they thought they had been interacting with.

Venturing into the world of online social networking is fun and entertaining, but if we don't follow some simple rules, our families could be in real danger. These social networking sites attract all types of people, and with large groups of people come predators who are going to try to capitalize on the popularity of these sites for their gain. Because social networks rely so heavily on trust, it is a target-rich environment for con artists to find ways to steal our money, our identity, or to pose as us in order to steal those things from our online friends.

TYPES OF SOCIAL NETWORKS

Not all social networks are created equal. There are differences in the types of social networks available on the Web today. Some are more open than others and encourage the meeting of people who don't know each other, and others are more restrictive and are intended for keeping in touch with friends and family that you already know in person and are comfortable with. Some allow anyone to see your updates, photos, and posts, and others only allow your "friends" to see them.

While most social networking sites have settings that allow you to control who can read your updates, not many people actually change those settings. At the end of the day, you could set your privacy settings on just about any social networking site to be either very restrictive or wide open—but your choice may defeat the purpose of that particular social network, and thus restrict your ability to effectively make use of that social network.

So, while there are aspects of both restrictive and non-restrictive sites in virtually every social network, it is still fairly accurate to categorize social networks into two basic categories based on their purpose: 1. to keep in touch with friends, and 2. to meet and get to know people.

KEEP IN TOUCH WITH FRIENDS

The main idea behind these social networking sites is to stay updated on what's happening in the lives of people you know. You can post short descriptions of what you are thinking, what you are working on, where you're planning to go on vacation, and so on. You can upload pictures to these sites as well—so you could share images of your last family vacation, the latest renovations to your home, or the new baby that just arrived. Many of these types of social network sites have built-in chat capabilities and the ability to see which of your friends are currently online. They also have birthday reminders and other features that act on very personal data that we would not want strangers to have access to.

On these types of sites, you must connect with people in order to read their updates and access their personal data. In order to connect, both parties must agree to make the connection—in other words, they both have to say that they want to be connected. For example, I could request a connection with my children, but until they indicate that they know me and that they want to be connected to me, I cannot see their updates. Of course, security settings can be loosened so that anyone can see the updates, but connections must still be agreed to on both sides.

Examples of this type of Social Networking site are: Facebook.com, MySpace.com, LinkedIn.com, and Classmate.com, among others. The main danger of these types of sites is the fact that there is a high degree of trust inherent in connections. Since you believe you know the person already, you are more open with them and more apt to post personal information on your page. Remember that although the expectation is that you know all of your connections in real life, there is no way to enforce that—and your children could connect to anyone that requests a connection with them, whether they truly know them or not. Often a predator will request a connection, indicating that they have some common friends. Not all children are cautious enough to know that this may be a ploy, and they accept the connection, curious to find out who this person is. The predator now has access to plenty of personal information to begin their online relationship. It is important in this type of social network to only connect with those whom you truly already know in the physical world.

MEET AND GET TO KNOW PEOPLE

The main idea behind this type of social networking site is to expand your physical network and to meet people you don't know already. This is like an on-going, virtual meet-n-greet, where you can find people with similar interests and meet new friends. Some people use these kinds of sites to expand their influence in their chosen career or to help make a name for themselves in some specific area. Many public figures use these social networks to inform people of what they are doing. Many politicians are using them to keep their constituency informed of their activities on their behalf or to ask for feedback on a particular bill or initiative. Television and movie stars use these networks to maintain their fan base and to help keep their name on people's minds when they are between roles.

Examples of these types of sites would be Twitter.com and individual blogs.[5] On these sites, you cannot control who has access to your posts—they are available for anyone who is interested to read them. Twitter, for example, allows you to search for some individual by name and to sign up to follow him. Once you sign up, you receive all of that person's posts, or tweets, as Twitter calls them.[6] Similarly, if someone creates a blog, it is simply a web page that exists on the Internet where anyone in the world can go and read the content. While Twitter and most blog sites have settings to lock them down so that you have more control over who reads your posts, this, in effect, defeats the purpose of that particular social network.

The main danger of these sites is that people might post something they didn't intend to, and it is now available for everyone to see. I am on Twitter and have seen an example of this in the very recent past—a politician thought he was texting a friend but instead sent a message to all 1,500+ of his Twitter followers. The message divulged some not-yet-public information regarding his upcoming run for public office. Another example, more applicable to our children, would be more of a danger for people who are used to the "Keep in Touch With Friends" type of social networking site, and might post some very personal information on these other networks. Here again, this is just a gold mine for predators to learn about you.

<h2 style="text-align:center">WHAT TO DO</h2>

Both types of social networking sites are very useful and can be very effective tools for communicating in this digital world. They can reunite us with old friends, or they can help improve our career opportunities. When used correctly, they are powerful tools. So, while we don't necessarily need to shun social networks, we do need to know how to use them safely. Here are ten simple rules to follow when your family wants to join the social networking craze:

1. As a parent, set up an account for yourself and become "friends" with your children. This will allow you to periodically check their profile page so you can see everything that their other "friends" can see. Remember, it is not snooping when you are simply reading what they have posted for the rest of the world to see.

2. Check your children's online pages often—make sure they aren't posting too much personal information or inappropriate images or having inappropriate contact with people they don't know. And watch for duplicate pages—some children will create multiple social networking pages, one where they befriend their parent, and the real one that they use to communicate with everyone else. There are tools out there to help find these, but often a simple search for their name will locate the page—after all, they want their friends to find them, so they aren't going to hide the real page too well.

3. Review your child's chat sessions. This could be as simple as looking over their shoulder once in a while as they are interacting with their friends, or it could mean using some technology to log their chat sessions. Either way, it is important to know what they are chatting about online. This may sound drastic, but the fact is

that usually a predator will quickly direct the chat to the subject he is interested in—whether that is getting your child to reveal personal information, or getting him to discuss inappropriate activities. Adults can usually detect these predators faster than a child can. While some may feel this is an invasion of their child's privacy, it is no different than overhearing a phone conversation or hearing them interact with friends in the next room. Figuring out how much to involve yourself in your children's online activities is just another effective parenting skill you will need to learn in order to keep them safe.

4. Instruct your children about what data is not appropriate to reveal online—things like birth dates, home addresses, social security numbers, account numbers, and so forth. Make sure they don't reveal information that a predator would be able to use to either locate them or steal their identities—or yours.

5. Review the images that they post to these sites. Make sure they are not posting inappropriate images, pictures of your home or street, or images of their school. Anything that can be used to identify them in the real world could be used by a predator to track them down. Images that are too personal could attract the attention of a predator.

6. Instruct your children that when they do post pictures and videos, they should ensure that only their online friends can see them. Usually social networking sites have settings regarding who can see your data—you can set them so everyone can see your online content or just your friends. A good rule of thumb is to only allow your friends to see your pictures and videos. This usually keeps them out of sight of online predators. Ask your children to help you set the privacy settings for your page—this way, if they don't know how, you can learn together. Then, you can suggest that they set the privacy settings for their accounts as well.

7. Review their friends lists with your children regularly. Make sure they actually know each person in real life. Ask them how they know this friend and where they met them. Instruct them not to connect with friends that they meet online, and *never* to meet anyone in person that they only know from online interactions.

8. Watch for impersonators. One of the problems with social networking sites is the immediate trust level that you have with

your "friends." It has become popular for predators to impersonate someone online, and befriend others using this fake identity. Watch for strange conversations or inappropriate requests—such as someone asking for money or for your passwords, account numbers, or other such personal data. As mentioned earlier, these requests will usually come via online chats. Teach your children to bring any strange online conversations to your attention.

9. Beware of the fun applications that are spread online through these social networks. Usually, these applications will require your permission to run—but they are usually promoted as something fun—have a virtual water balloon fight or send an online card. In order to access the application, you have to give permission for the application to access your personal information—this is a warning sign. Predators will use these innocuous looking applications to gain access to your profile and will then either try to impersonate you to your friends in an attempt to steal their money, or will attempt to run malicious software on your computer that will then steal your data. While these applications can be fun, they can also be extremely dangerous.

10. Finally, instruct your children to remember who they are and that they carry your family name; their comments will reflect on you and on them for many years to come. The Internet provides a false sense of anonymity, and this sometimes leads us to post comments or pictures that might not accurately represent us. We think that only our friends will ever read this or see this image. Remember that anything that is posted online could resurface somewhere else in the future. We need to be respectful in our comments and not post anything online that we would not want posted on the bulletin board at church, at the post office, or in any other public location. Even if our comments are posted only to our friends, once it is online it, is in the public domain.

By following these simple rules, we can keep our families safe while allowing them to participate in the global conversation that is happening on social networks.

Notes

1. M. Russell Ballard, "Sharing the Gospel Using the Internet," *Ensign*, July 2008, 58–63.

2. http://abcnews.go.com/technology/Story?id=3828525&page
   =1.
3. http://web-strategis.com/blog/2009/01/11/a-collection-of-
   social-network-stats-for-2009/.
4. http://ksl.com/index/php?nid-148&sid=5638053.
5. The term "blog" comes from "Web Log."
6. If you are on Twitter, feel free to follow me—I can be found at
   www.Twitter.com/KenKnapton.

9
PEER-TO-PEER
FILE SHARING

"In ancient times, a fortress required regular inspections to ensure that no weak spots developed that an enemy could take advantage of, and guards in the watchtowers ensured that no enemy could approach undetected.... By establishing a security system of our own, we can prevent the enemy from finding and exploiting weaknesses in our family fortress through which he could gain access to, and harm, our most precious treasure, our family."[1]

Horacio A. Tenorio

PEER-TO-PEER NETWORKS

In recent years peer-to-peer, or P2P, file-sharing technology has become quite popular. This has mainly been driven by the soaring popularity of digital music and video players. The concept behind a P2P application is that it allows users to easily share files via the Internet, making it very easy to obtain content for digital players. Rather than having to convert a file from your CD to the digital format that your player supports, you can simply use a P2P application to find a digital copy, then download it. There are several P2P applications on the market today, and most of them are free of charge.

LEGAL AND SECURITY ISSUES WITH P2P APPLICATIONS

From a security and safety standpoint, there are several areas of concern with P2P applications. Of course, there are also the legal issues, since copy-right laws can be easily ignored and bypassed using these applications. One of the first P2P applications, Napster, was forced to close down operations due to copyright infringement allegations. However, Napster is operating again, now within the bounds of the current copyright laws. This does not mean, however, that copyrighted material is no longer being shared illegally; it simply means that these companies are not liable for possible infringements by the users of those applications because of the way that the application operates. There are some subtle legal issues regarding copy-right liability that can be easily addressed by the developers and operators of these applications to allow them to operate within the legal boundaries.

P2P APPLICATIONS AND CONTENT FILTERS

Apart from the legal issues surrounding P2P applications, there are significant security concerns. In my opinion, these applications are the single most effective way to bypass the security measures that are put in place to protect your computer and your family. These applications are designed to provide a direct pathway into your computer from any other computer in the world. The protocols that are used are not normally monitored by any of the security or filter applications, which means that by using a P2P application you are opening your computer, and your home, to complete strangers and allowing them to directly place anything they want on your system.

> Installing a Peer-to-Peer file-sharing application on your computer is like adding an unlocked back door directly into your children's room. Most of your Internet safety mechanisms are bypassed, inviting complete strangers to send files directly to your computer.

In Chapter 7 we discussed the concept of a filter being like a guard that is standing at the door, ensuring that inappropriate content is not allowed into our home. Installing a P2P application is analogous to opening a window and installing a conveyor belt that can bring content into your home without that content being reviewed by the guard.[2] Worse yet, this virtual conveyor belt is potentially connected to every internet-enabled home in the world. Anyone can simply place a package on that conveyor belt, and it is allowed into our homes without inspection by any control-ling entity, including our filters. To make things even more concerning, there are currently no laws managing the content of these applications. This means that people can create videos that are extremely graphic in nature, place them on this conveyor belt, and then have the video promptly delivered directly into your home, completely bypassing your filter. As a matter of fact, one of the primary uses of peer-to-peer applications is to share child pornography.

Imagine this scenario: Your child installs a conveyor belt into your home and then sends out a request for a stuffed teddy bear. Within seconds, packages begin arriving on the conveyor belt, all different sizes and colors. Some look brand new, and others are in very old and worn boxes. Each one says, "Stuffed Teddy Bear," but some of the labels are hand-written and others are professionally typed. Your young child lights up like its Christmas morning—he's so excited to open these boxes and find the perfect teddy bear. The first box he opens has a stuffed dog instead of a teddy bear. Not exactly what he had asked for, but he can simply open another. The next box contains a teddy bear, but it is purple—he really wanted a brown one. So he keeps opening box after box, looking for the right teddy bear. Then he opens one that contains a live rattle snake, or a scorpion, or a skunk, or . . . well, you get the idea.

In the physical world, you would never actually allow your children to accept things like this from strangers—the dangers are simply too obvious. If your child really wanted that teddy bear, you would simply take him to the store to buy one. The virtual counterpart to this story has dangers that are just as real: video files could arrive on your computer directly from a stranger's machine, marked as innocuous content that your children have requested. However, these files might contain code that will install malware, spyware, viruses or anything else that the creator of that file wants to drop onto your machine. They could also send any video they want—which could be anything from a bad practical joke to extremely graphic sexual or violent content which you would never want your child to see. Because this comes into your home on the P2P conveyor belt, your filter has no power to protect your children from this unwanted content.

All too often, our lack of understanding of this technology causes us to back away and allow our children to manage the technology without any supervision. We don't believe that they would seek out inappropriate things, so we don't get involved in trying to stifle their use of technology. What we are missing, however, is the fact that in today's digital world, this content comes looking for us—we don't need to seek it out.

What To Do

➤ Unless you have a valid need for these applications, I would suggest just removing all P2P applications that are installed on your system. And understand that there are very few, if any, valid reasons for P2P applications.

➤ Set your filter to block P2P applications and do so at the protocol level if your filter supports it. With the P2P applications blocked, you can always override the block if someone in your home has a valid need to use one, and it can be done with your supervision.

➤ If you really want to ensure that these applications cannot ever work, even with an override password, check with your Internet service provider to see if they can close down any P2P ports. Usually, you can close down everything but the ports needed to run web browsers. Your Internet Service Provider (ISP) should be able to answer any questions you have about this.

➤ You may also be able to close down the protocols within your own home by configuring your router to disallow traffic from those ports. This too is something that your ISPs technical support should be able to help you with.

➤ You could also close down the ports on the local firewall (most have the ability to be configured at the port level). Unless you are familiar with this technology, I would not suggest doing this yourself. However, you could find a friend, neighbor, or local computer store employee who might be able to help you get this configured.

➤ If you do allow P2P applications on your computer, keep an eye on the application's download directory. P2P applications have a cache directory in which they store all of their downloaded videos and music files. The cache directory is usually configured within the P2P application, itself, so you can set it to whatever location you want on your computer. You can then check that location regularly to see what has been downloaded. While this is not the best method for keeping track of what comes onto your machine, it is better than having free, unrestricted, unmonitored access to all of the content on P2P systems.

➤ If you are going to allow P2P applications on your computer, check the security settings to ensure that only one directory on your computer is configured to share files. Often these applications are configured to allow full access to all files on your system, again providing a gold mine for anyone who wants to steal your identity and your money.

Notes:

1. Horacio A. Tenorio, "Let us Build Fortresses," *Ensign*, Nov. 1994, 23.

2. This is because the P2P applications operate on their own protocols. Each P2P application could potentially have its own protocol, although many are now making use of a handful of common protocols designed for this purpose.

10
EMAIL

"May the Lord bless all of us not to be fooled by illusions created by the devil."[1]

Gene R. Cook

EMAIL COMMUNICATION

Email is fast becoming the communication method of choice for U.S. adults (but not children—they prefer texting and online chatting). According to the results of a new study, 60 percent of U.S. Internet users prefer reading email to reading ordinary post and 34 percent prefer sending email to making a telephone call.[2] According to Paul Ottellini, President of Intel Corporation, over 1 million people send email every day, and this number is expected to rise over time.

SPAM

As with any other popular technologies, there are some dangers associated with email. In January 2008, the rate of spam (unsolicited email messages) to legitimate email was 63.28 percent;[3] in other words, over half of the messages you receive every day are unsolicited, unwanted junk that is difficult, if not impossible, to regulate in an effective manner. We don't ask for

The term "Spam" became associated with email when the first unsolicited message was sent from one co-worker to another as a joke. The content of the message: the "Spam song" from the famous Monty Python skit.

spam, and we have no idea what these messages will actually contain.

Much like mass mailings to our home mailboxes, the purveyors of spam send mass mailings of email messages, usually trying to either sell us something or promote some website. Obviously, this is a much more cost-effective way for advertisers to get their content into our homes because they don't have to pay any postage fees. However, on the receiving end, the receiver actually ends up bearing much of the cost of the spam, since we have to pay for the Internet access into our homes, as well as our email system. Most email systems now come with built-in spam filtering to help keep these unwanted messages from our inbox, but spammers are doing everything they can to bypass those filters and get their content into our inbox. As quickly as the anti-spam technology picks up on one of their tricks, spammers come up with a new one. The latest trick is to send you messages from your own email address, so the anti-spam programs cannot simply reject the email.

TYPES OF EMAIL LISTS USED FOR SPAM

There are two kinds of email lists that spammers use: *confirmed* and *unconfirmed*. The distinction is important to understand if you are going to keep your inbox (and your children's inboxes) as spam-free as possible. These two types of email lists are described in more detail below.

Confirmed addresses are those that have been proven to actually have been read by a human being—in other words, the email address is confirmed to belong to an actual person. You might ask how a spammer could know this. It is because, at one time, the spammer sent some type of innocuous message to this email address, and the recipient clicked on a link, ran a program, replied to the message, or in some other way responded to the spam. As soon as you respond to a spam message in any way, your email address is confirmed to the spammer via a simple report-ing mechanism.

An **unconfirmed** list contains addresses that have not been proven to actually go anywhere, and may or may not actually lead to someone's inbox. This list could be compiled by using a company list that was leaked to the public or a set of email addresses that were mined from the Internet somewhere or through any number of other ways that email addresses can be obtained. These addresses have not been proven to actually make it into a human being's inbox.

Spammers actually purchase email lists from people. They pay a premium for confirmed addresses, whereas unconfirmed addresses are discounted. Consequently, there are many people who send messages just to try to confirm email addresses so they can make more money when they sell their list. They send jokes, email chain letters, or anything else that might entice someone to respond in some way. These messages are usually benign and will do no harm to your machine or your data, but it will confirm your email address to the sender, who will then sell your address to spammers. Then the bad stuff starts inundating your inbox. Unfortunately, our children often fall for these email tricks, as they are all-too-happy to reply to a message informing people about their favorite color and too naive to know that Bill Gates isn't going to send them a check if they forward an email. Rather than just deleting a message, they pass it along and usually include some sort of personal information that we would rather they did not share with the public, including their names, home towns, and so forth. Children inadvertently play right into the hands of spammers.

While some governments try to regulate spam, the truth is that it is very difficult to track down the purveyors of this content, and even more difficult to actually hold them accountable. Some spammers have been caught and charged with crimes in the United States, but most go unpunished.

There are some regulations regarding email messages, such as the rule that you must include a way to unsubscribe from an email list when you send unsolicited messages to people. Unfortunately, spammers don't really care about abiding by the rules, and they use their "remove me from this list" request as a way to confirm your email address. Rather than removing you from the list, they move your email address from their unconfirmed list to their confirmed list. So instead of reducing the spam in your inbox, you have just increased your chances of getting more spam.

EMAIL AND CONTENT FILTERS

It is also important to remember that email travels on a different protocol than standard browser content, so email content usually bypasses your filter. It sneaks past your guard, unbeknownst to you.

Once again, we have the false sense of security that because we have installed a filter, our children cannot see anything inappropriate; and once again, we are wrong. Images are often embedded in spam and can be viewed by anyone who opens the email message. There is usually a link in the message where the individual could click to go see more of this content, and if your child did click on that link, the chances are high that your filter would kick in at that point and prohibit the visit to the website—but the damage would have already been done by the images that were embedded in the email message itself.

Spam email can include anything from pharmaceutical messages trying to convince us that we need to increase the size of certain body parts (sometimes with images of those parts), to full-blown, hardcore pornography. Along with embedding images in the message itself, spammers can also send anything they want as an attachment—once again bypassing our filter. Attachments can include images, videos, applications . . . virtually anything.

Spammers don't usually target any specific demographic—after all, the only thing they have is an email address. They don't know, or care, whether the person who eventually receives the email is a child or an adult, or whether the individual has any desire to even see the content they are sending. While there are laws against distributing "adult" material to minors, these spammers are hardly ever caught, and most are willing to take the risk. They just send their messages en masse and hope that even a small percentage will click on the embedded links.

The reason that spam is such a problem is that people respond to it. We click on the links, respond to messages, or do something else that pulls us into the trap. We are simply too gullible as a people. When something is written down and sent to our inbox, we can't stand to think that we might miss out on some great benefit by ignoring the message. The best thing we can do with spam messages is simply delete them without opening the message. Just about any other reaction will only add our email address to some spammer's confirmed list.

How to Protect Your Email Address

So, how do these mass emailers get our email address in the first place? There are actually some legal and morally ethical ways to obtain these lists in addition to some very unscrupulous methods. Anyone who accesses the Internet and who has an email address should understand this, and should protect his email address as best he can.

Here are a few suggestions for how to do this:

Email Chain Letters

The speed of light is like molasses in winter compared to a viral Internet chain letter. Nothing travels faster than a "tell me about yourself" email sent to teenagers or some story about a poor child in a far off country who will die unless this message is forwarded to as many people as possible in the next twelve hours.

Regardless of what the chain letter is, the temptation to forward it on is just too much for our young children to resist. They send it to all of their friends, and the friends send it on again. Unfortunately, as they forward the message over and over, all of the email addresses of the people who received it are listed in the message—which is a gold mine for spammers. Over the course of just a day or two, each message could end up containing hundreds of email addresses. All a spammer needs to do is harvest the addresses from the message, and he instantly has plenty of unwitting victims to whom he can send his spam. Worse yet, some of these messages contain malicious code that will mine your machine for email addresses and send them directly to the spammer, giving them not only your address, but that of all of your family and friends as well.

Apart from causing more spam, the "tell me about yourself" messages have another potentially dangerous side effect. Internet predators who find a message like this one in their inboxes are instantly provided with all of the information they need to start a relationship with your child. They can use this information to make your children think they are also a young child who just happens to have the same interests as your child does.

Web Pages

Anyone who places his email address on a web page is essentially handing it to hundreds of spammers. It is trivially simple to write a computer application that can scour the Web looking for email addresses posted on public web pages. Those addresses are then easily dumped into a database and used for spam. Of course, the popularity of user-generated content and social networking sites compounds this problem, as people now often post their email addresses on their personal web pages or blogs.

This is the reason for the proliferation of confirmation screens, where you are shown a graphic of characters and asked to type the characters into a text field on a website. As annoying as this step is, it is designed to prevent spammers from obtaining email addresses. Applications that scour the Internet for email addresses cannot read these screens, and thus they cannot enter the required text. Spammers are getting very smart, however, and are even finding ways around this. The way they do this is quite technical, but essentially they convince people to enter the information for them by posting the confirmation screen on their own websites, and then passing the answer on to the original website. As long as people post their email addresses on websites, spammers will figure out a way to access them.

Company Email Lists

Before you provide your email address to any company (whether it's to sign up for their newsletter, to receive updates on their latest product releases, or anything else), check their privacy policy. By law (at least in the United States), all companies are supposed to make their privacy policies available to you before they can accept your email address.

Sometimes even scrupulous and ethical companies decide to make some extra cash by selling their collection of email addresses to other companies. This may be for valid reasons. For example, two companies may have a symbiotic relationship and need to reach the same customers. However, once your email address is shared among companies without your knowledge, you have no control if one of them decides to sell the list to a company that turns out to be nothing more than a front for spammers.

If the company to which you are about to provide your email address does not have an express privacy policy of not sharing its email addresses, you may want to think twice about providing your email address.

WHAT TO DO

➤ Don't ever respond to chain letters, *ever*. Period. And teach your children not to either. No one is tracking the number of times a certain message was forwarded to calculate how large of a check to send you, no one will be saved based on how many times a message is forwarded, and your friends don't need to get an email to learn more about your likes and dislikes—they can simply ask you. Don't even open this type of message, as this can send a response to the spammer without your knowledge. Just delete them and move on with your life. If you ever wonder about the validity of a message, just search for it on snopes.com. I have never found this website to be incorrect with regard to Internet hoaxes.

➤ Don't freely give out your email address to any company without first reading its privacy policy. Ensure that the company is going to treat your email address with the same care that it would treat your credit card number. And, if it isn't, don't give your information to it. You can live without that newsletter or product update. The danger is simply too high.

➤ Some email programs have an option to turn off images. Look into your email package and see if this is an option for you. You may want to turn off images for your children's email accounts. Usually, you can turn the images back on when you are there to supervise. So if they are actually sent some cool picture from a friend they can still see it, with your permission.

➤ Teach your children not to open any messages from people they don't know and reiterate to them the dangers of opening attachments. In fact, there are some email packages for children that can be configured to disallow attachments altogether—one such site is zoobuh.com. Consider making use of one of these email services.

Notes:

1. Gene R. Cook, "Spiritual Guides for Teachers of Righteousness," *Ensign*, May 1982, 25.
2. As reported by Americangreetings.com
3. As reported by ieInternet.com, http://www.ieinternet.com/content/view/33/.

11
MOBILE COMPUTING AND CELL PHONES

"This is an age of digital information.... Literally at the click of a button, we can browse through the digitized libraries of universities, museums, government agencies, and research institutions located throughout the world. A worldwide web of electronic connections now moves data at ever-increasing speed and volume along what we call the information superhighway."[1]

Joseph B. Wirthlin

THE MOBILE INTERNET

The Internet is growing at a phenomenal rate. The amount of new technical information is currently doubling every two years. It is estimated that by 2010 it will double every seventy-two hours. The Internet is fast becoming the preferred delivery mechanism for all data, and we (the consumers of that data) are demanding that

"We're now in the midst of the largest opportunity to redefine consumer electronics and entertainment since the introduction of the television ... Increasingly, computing and communications are coming together, bringing a new level of capabilities and intelligence to the Internet experience. The personal Internet of tomorrow will [deliver] the information you want, when you want it, how you want, wherever you are."

Paul Otellini, keynote speaker
International Consumer Electronics Show

111

it be more accessible to us whenever and wherever we are. It is estimated that we will generate more new, unique information this year than has been generated in the past 5,000 years.[2] With the addition of new mobile devices, content on the Internet can reach us wherever we are, whenever we want it.

MOBILE INTERNET DEVICES

The Internet is becoming more mobile at an exponential rate. Cell phones, digital music players, laptops—they are all becoming Internet aware, allowing us full access to the myriad of information available on the Internet anytime, anywhere. In 2007, there were more than 27 million laptops sold worldwide,[3] and Paul Ottelini, President of Intel Corporation, reports that current estimates indicate that laptop sales will double every year through 2012. He also predicts that in 2009 laptop sales will surpass desktop sales worldwide.[4] This would be staggering in and of itself, but when you consider that the laptop is no longer the primary mobile Internet device, you realize that the Internet is, indeed, extremely mobile these days. Consider the sales of Internet-enabled cell phones and other MIDs (Mobile Internet Devices); clearly the Internet is no longer restricted to your home computer. Our children use these technologies every day and can access Internet content any time they wish.

Text messaging is becoming the communication mechanism of choice for an entire generation. It is estimated that the number of text messages sent daily currently exceeds the population of the planet. It is not uncommon to see a group of teenagers sitting together, carrying on conversations via text messaging rather than talking to each other. In fact, a 2008 study found that the typical U.S. mobile phone subscriber sends or receives more text messages per month than phone calls via his cell phone.[5] In a separate study, done by Harris Interactive, teens indicated that a cell phone ranks second only to clothes in determining social status, and 42 percent of those studied said they could text blindfolded! That same study indicated that 1 of 3 teens regularly browses the Web on his phone.[6]

DANGERS ASSOCIATED WITH MOBILE INTERNET

There are plenty of dangers related to Internet-enabled mobile devices. The fact that personal contact is removed and our children are interacting with a device, rather than a person, often causes them to do and say things that they would never have the courage or audacity to do in person. The local news stations in Utah have recently reported the discovery of elementary-school aged children sharing naked images of themselves with each other via their camera phones. It seems that these children took pictures of themselves and text-messaged the image to their friends—and this is a phenomenon that is not limited to Utah.

In fact, this has become such a popular thing to do that it has been given a name: "sexting." Not only is sexting inappropriate, it is actually illegal when it is young children doing it, as these images of young children are technically considered to be child pornography, and is punishable by the very strict U.S. laws prohibiting the possession and distribution of child pornography. Quite often these images are forwarded beyond the intended recipient, and the original sender actually becomes a victim as his image is spread across his school and among his friends.

Even without collusion from their friends, our children can easily obtain inappropriate images on their mobile Internet devices. There are subscription services that will send pornographic images to your cell phone on a regular basis. All that is required to subscribe to this service is to send a text message to a specific number, and then you will immediately start receiving extremely graphic images directly to your mobile device. Utah Attorney General Mark Shurtleff refers to this as "porn in a pocket." Parents need to understand that when they provide their children with an Internet-enabled cell phone, they are opening up the entire Internet to that child, wherever and whenever he wants to use it.

MOBILE DEVICES AND CONTENT FILTERS

Unfortunately, the technology to track, monitor, and filter this content has not yet caught up to the trend of mobile Internet access. As we learned in Chapter 7, filters only work when the content flows through the filtering device prior to reaching its destination. When you install a filter on your home computer, it only protects the content flowing onto *that* computer. Even if you install a gateway filter on your wireless network in your home, it will not protect the cell phones being used in your home because these devices operate on a completely different network and the content never flows through your filter. Even configuring a proxy filter is useless for these devices because they operate on their own network and cannot be configured to access the Internet through a proxy.

Until filtering technology catches up to the mobile Internet device trend, our children are at risk of coming into contact with inappropriate material—or worse yet seeking it out—without the fear of being detected by the filters installed on our home computing devices to protect against such exposure.

MOBILE INTERNET DEVICES AND MULTITASKING

Apart from the dangers of unrestricted access to all Internet content, there is another, more subtle danger for our children. A recent study published by Russell A. Poldrack, professor of behavioral neuroscience at the University of California, Los Angeles, shows that multitasking actually has a negative effect on learning.[7] Mobile Internet devices, like cell phones, create a multitasking environment for our children, whether it be text-messaging while doing homework or searching the Internet while sitting in the classroom. In the Harris Interactive study mentioned above, when teens were asked why they like to text, 53 percent of females and 38 percent of males indicated that they text because it allows them to multitask.

Dr. Poldrack's study provides scientific evidence that when we attempt to multitask while learning a new concept, we perform worse than when we focus only on that task. While this seems like common sense, there is a common misconception in today's culture that we are more productive when we multitask. Dr. Poldrack refers to this as "the myth of multitasking"—a myth which his research has proven incorrect. To see just how dangerous this could be to our society, walk into just about any high school today and count the number of students who have their mobile Internet devices in their hands while their teacher is instructing them.

WHAT TO DO

➢ Images that are sent to a cell phone are usually stored on them. Spot check your children's phones. Look at the images on the phone and be sure you know how they are using it. Watch the phone bill to see how many images they are sending and receiving each month.

➢ There are plenty of warning signs in the text messages that our children receive. Spot check these as well to see who your children text most often. Ask them about these people: who they are, how they met, how long they have known them. Predators know how to get to our children, and if they can make it onto our children's phone contact list, they have made a significant in-road with our children.

➢ Watch the phone bill. Look for spikes in text messages coming from numbers you don't know or from services that may, in reality, transmit illicit content such as a daily pornographic image.

➢ Use the parental controls on these devices. As limited as they may be now, they are better than nothing. And eventually the technology will improve.

➢ Most cell phone companies will allow you to turn off web browsing and other features if you ask them. Limiting cell phone usage to only phone calls and text messages, without images or web browsing, goes a long way toward making cell phones safer for our children.

➢ Learn the texting lingo so you can understand your children's text messages when you see them. NetLingo has a great listing of acronyms and shorthand used when texting and chatting. You can find it here: **http://www.netlingo.com/acronyms.php**

Notes

1. Joseph B. Wirthlin, "Windows of Light and Truth," *Ensign*, Nov. 1995, 75–78.
2. www.ShiftHappens.org.
3. Nicholas Negroponte, NECC keynote address
4. Paul Ottelini, Keynote address at the UTC Hall of Fame event, Fall 2007.
5. http://www.nielsenmobile.com/html/press%20releases/TextVersusCalls.html.
6. Harris Interactive, "A Generation Unplugged," Sept 12, 2008, http://www.ctia.org/advocacy/research/index.cfm/AID/11483.
7. Karin Foerde, Barbara J. Knowlton, and Russell A. Poldrack. "Modulation of Competing Memory Systems by Distraction," Department of Psychology and Brain Research Institute, University of California, June 9, 2006.

12
TELEVISION AND VIDEO GAMES

"Children learn through gentle direction and persuasive teaching. They search for models to imitate, knowledge to acquire, things to do, and teachers to please."[1]

Thomas S. Monson

TELEVISION AND THE INTERNET

It used to be that television was much like the dumb terminals[2] of old, where the monitor simply acted as a medium to display data that was actually housed elsewhere and transmitted to the monitor for users to view. Today, the line between computers and television is quickly diminishing. More television networks are making their programming available via the Internet, and with the advent of digital video recording (DVR) technology, our televisions now have the ability to store content just like our computers do. Many of these DVRs have the ability to set recordings via the Internet. It will not be long before there is no difference between a computer connected to the Internet and your television. The TV will simply be another device that receives

"What is placed in the child's brain during the first six years of life is probably there to stay.... If you put misinformation into his brain during [this period], it is extremely difficult to erase it."

Dr. Glenn Doman, *How to Teach Your Baby to Read* (1964, 46–47).

117

content over the Internet. I suspect that we will soon be able to interact with our television programs in much the same way that we interact with content from the Web today. This is already apparent with DVRs that allow us to pause and rewind live TV. I also believe that we will be able to pick and choose the content to display on our televisions in much the same way that we can choose which websites to visit. Moreover, as more television content is made available on the Web, it is also made available to every Internet device, including mobile and hand-held devices. Television programming is no longer limited to our living rooms.

IMPLICATIONS OF TELEVISION AND INTERNET CONVERGENCE

While this all sounds great on the surface, there are some very serious implications to this technology. Regulating television programming and an increased availability of inappropriate content are only a couple of the concerns with this transition. As we have seen with mobile internet devices, filtering technologies and appropriate laws to regulate content generally lag behind the availability of inappropriate content.

Hollywood knows this and understands the implications of making their content available via the Web. In fact, one of the primary issues behind the writers' strike of late 2007 and early 2008 was that, based on the concept that more and more content was legally moving to the Web, the writers did not feel they were being properly compensated for content that was being distributed over the Internet. In the larger picture, we, as families, need to understand that as more content is made available to web-enabled devices there is more content out there that is not regulated in the same way that it is when it is sent through the airwaves. Similar to how DVDs today offer "unrated" versions of popular movies, the Internet provides the means for Hollywood producers to distribute unrated or director's cut versions of popular television programs.

REGULATION OF TELEVISION PROGRAMMING

It is important to understand the distinction between television and the Internet when it comes to the law. Since the Internet deals with digital content, it is very easy for producers and directors to make a new cut of a television episode that may not fall within FCC guidelines and make it available over the Web. Since the episode is hosted in the Internet, and not sent over the airwaves, the FCC has no control over it. For more information on FCC regulations, see the *Adult Content on Television* section below.

As of early 2008, broadcasting unrated versions of mainstream television episodes has not yet become a popular practice, but it is something that parents need to be aware of as a possibility and watch for. Be careful when viewing television content that has been posted on the Internet and make sure that it is the same version that was broadcast over the airwaves. I personally believe that it will not be long before networks start offering multiple versions of their television programs on the Internet: the broadcast version and the "unrated" version, much like DVDs do for movies. If we are not watchful and if we freely allow our children to watch television shows on the Internet, assuming that the same FCC regulations apply, we could have a very rude awakening in the near future. The myriad of scantily clad women and sexually explicit content allowed on late-night TV is nothing compared to what is currently legal on the Internet.

VIOLENCE ON TELEVISION AND VIDEO GAMES

We also face a great danger with regard to the amount of violence that our children are exposed to in their entertainment today. Dr. Victor B. Cline said: "The amount of violence a child sees at 7 predicts how violent he will be at 17, 27, and 37. . . . Children's minds are like banks—whatever you put in, you get back 10 years later with interest." He indicated that violent television teaches children, step by step, "how to commit violent acts, and it desensitizes them to the horror of such behavior and to the feelings of victims." In Dr. Cline's opinion, America is suffering from "an explosion of interpersonal violence like we have never seen before. . . . The violence is because of violence in our entertainment."[3]

As I have talked in different venues on this subject, it is clear that some parents are not convinced that aggressive behaviors can be learned from violence on television and in video games. Many of the television programs aimed at children are extremely violent, especially some of the cartoons, they argue. Many of us simply brush it off, rationalizing that this is just how it is and that every child is exposed to this level of violence. In a now-famous study referred to as the Bobo doll study, Dr. Albert Bandura found that simply viewing violent behavior can indeed lead children to model that behavior. He conducted his study in 1961 with a group of twenty-four children between three and six years of age. He studied each child individually, to ensure that he was observing the behavior of the individual, and not the mob mentality of a group. The intent of the study was to see if the behavior of an adult would affect the way that these children played with different toys. The center piece of this experiment was a Bobo doll—an inflatable doll that stood about five feet tall.

The children were placed in a room with an adult who simply played with a tinker toy set for about ten minutes, then they were brought into another room where an adult pounded on the Bobo doll with a mallet for about ten minutes. The children were then allowed to play with the toys by themselves. The study became very controversial, especially with TV stations, because it showed that the children would, indeed, model the extremely aggressive behavior of beating on the Bobo doll with just about anything they could find. As it turned out, they not only physically, but verbally abused this doll based on the modeled behavior they saw from their adult playmate. In Bandura's own words, "They added creative embellishments. One girl actually transformed a doll into a weapon of assault." In the video of this study, one can plainly see a tiny, well-dressed young girl pounding the doll, and then searching the room for other things to pummel it with. Even though the adult model in the study did not play with the toy gun, Bandura noted that "exposure to aggressive modeling increased attraction to guns, even though it was never modeled." These young children made the connection between violent behavior and guns on their own.

> "It was once widely believed that seeing others vent aggression would drain the viewer's aggressive drive ... exposure to aggressive modeling is hardly cathartic. Exposure to aggressive modeling increased attraction to guns, even though it was never modeled."
>
> **Dr. Albert Bandura**

Children model the behavior they see. How much violence and sexual activity are they exposed to on the television and in video games today? It is challenging to find a show on primetime television that doesn't have some sort of violent or sexual overtones—and it has become steadily more so since this study. Remember that Dr. Bandura's study was done in 1961, when it was taboo to show a married couple sharing a bed on television. (Recall the Dick Van Dyke Show where the bedroom had twin beds.) Today you cannot get through an episode of most primetime sitcoms without sexual innuendos or overt references, and you cannot watch many dramas without extreme violence. As these shows become available on the Internet, where the content is no longer regulated by the FCC, they will become an even greater danger to our children. We need to be very careful about what we allow our children to watch, especially in their formative years.

In her analysis of Dr. Bandura's work, Christine Van De Velde wrote:

> [Dr.] Bandura demonstrated [that] exposure to TV violence can produce at least four effects. First, it teaches aggressive styles of conduct. Second, it weakens restraints against aggression by glamorizing violence. When good triumphs over evil violently, viewers are even more strongly influenced. Third, it habituates and desensitizes reactions to cruelty. And finally, it shapes our images of reality; for example, only 10 percent of major crimes in society are violent, but on TV, 77 percent of major crimes are violent, which has the effect of making people more fearful of becoming crime victims. "Children and adults today have unlimited opportunities to learn the whole gamut of homicidal conduct from TV within the comfort of their homes," notes Bandura.[4]

Of particular concern is the fact that even though good triumphs over evil in the end, doing so with violence only increases the problem of desensitizing violent behavior and teaches our children that violence is a perfectly acceptable way to resolve society's problems. Add to this the video games where children take on a persona that is inflicting violent behavior on others, and we can start to see an epidemic of violence in a generation of children.

From Columbine High School in Colorado to Virginia Tech in Virginia and Trolley Square in Utah—all across the country our young people seem to believe that violence is the only way to solve their personal problems. We cannot dismiss the association between this behavior and extremely violent television, movies, and video games. Since the terrible attack on Columbine High school, several studies have shown that there is indeed a correlation between violent video games and violence in real life. In years past, children with psychological problems would hurt or kill themselves—today they will hurt or kill others, and then themselves. There can be no doubt that violence on television and in video games has a very dangerous effect on our children.

ADULT CONTENT ON TELEVISION

What used to be taboo on television, such as showing a married couple sharing a bed, is now common, and the television industry is constantly trying to move the dial toward more and more edgy content. The only thing that has slowed their efforts is the Federal Communications Commission (FCC), which is charged with overseeing such transmissions. The FCC is responsible for maintaining the integrity of broadcast television and radio; however, it does not have authority to regulate the Internet. With regard to television and radio, the FCC operates under title 18 of the United States Code, Section 1464, which prohibits the utterance of "any obscene, indecent or profane language by means of radio communication."[5] According to current statute and case law, this indecent material and profane language is only prohibited between the hours of 6 AM and 10 PM. The FCC does not actively censor material but rather acts as an enforcement agency, monitoring and ensuring that the law is upheld by the broadcasters.

The FCC operates under the United State Supreme Court's interpretation of the word "obscene" when enforcing the law. The Supreme Court uses a three-prong test to define obscenity:

1. An average person, applying contemporary community standards, must find that the material, as a whole, appeals to the prurient interest (i.e., material having a tendency to excite lustful thoughts);
2. The material must depict or describe, in a patently offensive way, sexual conduct specifically defined by applicable law; and
3. The material, taken as a whole, must lack serious literary, artistic, political, or scientific value.[6]

In making this interpretation, the Supreme Court has made it clear that this test is designed to cover hard-core pornography. As we have all witnessed, Hollywood is only too happy to test those bounds and try to shift the "community standard" used as the litmus test in this description. If they can get the general public to accept something as not obscene, then they have shifted the community standard, and what was once illegal now becomes accepted.

As stated above, the FCC monitors television and radio broadcasts, but its standards do not apply to the Internet. But, what about cable television? The FCC's website answers this question:

> In the past, the FCC has enforced the indecency and profanity

prohibitions only against conventional broadcast services, not against subscription programming services such as cable and satellite. However, the prohibition against obscene programming applies to subscription programming services at all times.

This begs the question regarding the difference between "indecent" and "obscene." The website goes on to distinguish between obscenity and indecent programming as follows:

> ***What makes material "indecent?"*** Indecent material contains sexual or excretory material that does not rise to the level of obscenity. For this reason, the courts have held that indecent material is protected by the First Amendment and cannot be banned entirely. It may, however, be restricted to avoid its broadcast during times of the day when there is a reasonable risk that children may be in the audience. The FCC has determined, with the approval of the courts, that there is a reasonable risk that children will be in the audience from 6 a.m. to 10 p.m., local time. Therefore, the FCC prohibits station licensees from broadcasting indecent material during that period.
>
> Material is indecent if, in context, it depicts or describes sexual or excretory organs or activities in terms patently offensive as measured by contemporary community standards for the broadcast medium. In each case, the FCC must determine whether the material describes or depicts sexual or excretory organs or activities and, if so, whether the material is "patently offensive."
>
> In our assessment of whether material is "patently offensive," context is critical. The FCC looks at three primary factors when analyzing broadcast material: (1) whether the description or depiction is explicit or graphic; (2) whether the material dwells on or repeats at length descriptions or depictions of sexual or excretory organs; and (3) whether the material appears to pander or is used to titillate or shock. No single factor is determinative. The FCC weighs and balances these factors because each case presents its own mix of these, and possibly other, factors.[7]

So, if you pay for television[8] (either cable or satellite), you need to stay informed regarding which channels you have. Even with the basic packages, some channels run adult-oriented, unedited content, especially if that content is deemed "artistic," which gets it past the legal definition of obscenity. The content, including commercials aired during non-adult shows, gets much more graphic at night during the "safe harbor" time period. Broadcasters take full advantage of this time. Consider then the implications of having full access to any show on television at any hour via the Internet. The late-night, adult shows that can only air after 10 PM are now just as available as Dora the Explorer or Sesame Street.

TELEVISION RATING SYSTEM

To assist parents in determining what content their children should be allowed to see, programs today use the following rating system:

- ➤ TV-Y, (All Children) found only in children's shows, means that the show is appropriate for all children
- ➤ TV-7, (Directed to Older Children) found only in children's shows, means that the show is most appropriate for children ages seven years old and up
- ➤ TV-G (General Audience) means that the show is suitable for all ages but is not necessarily a children's show
- ➤ TV-PG (Parental Guidance Suggested) means that parental guidance is suggested and that the show may be unsuitable for younger children (this rating may also include a V for violence, S for sexual situations, L for language, or D for suggestive dialogue
- ➤ TV-14 (Parents Strongly Cautioned) means that the show may be unsuitable for children under 14 (V, S, L, or D may accompany a rating of TV-14)
- ➤ TV-MA (Mature Audience Only) means that the show is for mature audiences only and may be unsuitable for children under 17 (V, S, L, or D may accompany a rating of TV-MA)

These ratings are useful from a technology perspective as they are embedded in the television program itself and allow parental control applications to read the rating and either block or allow access to that content based on the rating. Most televisions today, as well as cable and satellite providers, provide a way for parents to lock out shows based on the show's ratings. None of the Internet content filters on the market today support these ratings, but it most likely will not be long before they do.

VIDEO GAME RATING SYSTEM

The game market also has a rating system, called the "Entertainment Software Rating Board" system or ESRB. These ratings are given to software games that you install onto your computer or run in a game console like a Nintendo, Playstation, or Xbox. Many of the filters available for your computer can block games based on their ESRB ratings and most game consoles come with this ability built in. Game rental and sales stores are not supposed to sell or rent teen or mature games to children, but quite often they do, so you cannot assume that any game your children bring home is rated appropriately for their age group. Enforcing the ESRB rating on your computer and game console is really the best way to ensure that your children have access only to those games that are appropriate for their age group.

The ESRB ratings are as follows:[9]

EARLY CHILDHOOD

Titles rated **EC (Early Childhood)** have content that may be suitable for ages 3 and older. Contains no material that parents would find inappropriate.

EVERYONE

Titles rated **E (Everyone)** have content that may be suitable for ages 6 and older. Titles in this category may contain minimal cartoon, fantasy, or mild violence and/or infrequent use of mild language.

EVERYONE 10+

Titles rated **E10+ (Everyone 10 and older)** have content that may be suitable for ages 10 and older. Titles in this category may contain more cartoon, fantasy, or mild violence, mild language, and/or minimal suggestive themes.

TEEN

Titles rated **T (Teen)** have content that may be suitable for ages 13 and older. Titles in this category may contain violence, suggestive themes, crude humor, minimal blood, simulated gambling, and/or infrequent use of strong language.

MATURE

Titles rated **M (Mature)** have content that may be suitable for persons ages 17 and older. Titles in this category may contain intense violence, blood and gore, sexual content, and/or strong language.

ADULTS ONLY

Titles rated **AO (Adults Only)** have content that should only be played by persons 18 years and older. Titles in this category may include prolonged scenes of intense violence and/or graphic sexual content and nudity.

RATING PENDING
Titles listed as **RP (Rating Pending)** have been submitted to the ESRB and are awaiting final rating. (This symbol appears only in advertising prior to a game's release.)

ONLINE GAMING

The most popular gaming systems such as the Wii and Xbox are now online, allowing you to connect and interact with anyone else in the world who has the same game system and an Internet connection. Some even allow you to surf the Internet and include a built-in web browser. Many parents are not aware of this and allow their children to connect to the Internet via their game box. The overlooked implication, however, is that unless you have a gateway filter installed, this provides unfiltered Internet access from the one device that is most likely used primarily by the children in the home. To make matters worse, the tools that are used to monitor Internet access, chat logs, websites visited, and so forth are not yet available on these machines. This means that while you may vigilantly protect your children as they access the Internet from the computers in your home, you may have inadvertently opened up a direct line to all of the content on the Internet simply by purchasing a game box. Most of these game machines have the ability to lock down the Internet access, or at the very least, to turn off the browser so that one cannot use the machine to surf the Internet. This has no impact on the games or your children's ability to play online games; it simply turns off the ability to freely surf the Internet via the game box.

As we learned in Chapter 1, the FBI has stated that if your children hang out in chat rooms, they have a 100 percent chance of interacting with a child predator. Since all of the online games include the ability to chat among the participants, these games need to be considered as not much more than a very entertaining chat room. Remember that there is no way to tell who is really typing on the other end of a chat, and that Internet predators are going to hang out where you children are. Chatting in games is very dangerous. Predators hang out in the games to initiate chats with children. They make plans to meet back in the game at certain times of the day and strategize together regarding how to play the game. Predators are very patient; sometimes they build relationships over months before trying to arrange an in-person meeting. By then, the children feel they know this person—they have played with them, talked with them, learned about them. They believe they aren't meeting a stranger; they are going to meet one of their gaming friends, and maybe even in a very public place. Just like Alicia Kozakiewicz, whom we met in Chapter 2, our children's intentions may be innocuous but the consequences are not.

What To Do

- ➢ Turn off the Internet access on your gaming systems.
  - o Turn on the parental controls, so this cannot be turned back on without your knowledge.
- ➢ If you want your children to be able to play with friends online, then turn off the Internet browsing capability. Most gaming consoles allow you to turn off browsing but leave on gaming.
- ➢ Know who your children are playing with.
  - o Walk by when they are playing. Watch some of the chat messages. See how they communicate online.
  - o If they send a "POS" (parent over shoulder) message, or something similar, this is a warning sign. Find out why they feel the need to warn others that you are there.
- ➢ Talk to them about their online friends.
- ➢ Know what your children watch on TV.
- ➢ Use the parental controls. Most televisions, cable companies, and satellite companies have parental controls.
  - o Lock out certain channels completely.
  - o Lock out programming based on content or rating.
- ➢ Use the ESRB rating feature on your filter and game console.
- ➢ Limit television time.
- ➢ Beware of violence, even in cartoons. Children learn aggressive behavior from watching others.

Notes
1. Thomas S. Monson, "Teaching Our Children," *Ensign*, Oct. 2004, 2-7.
2. A "dumb terminal" was a monitor and keyboard that was connected to a main frame housed elsewhere. It was called a dumb terminal because it had no way to store data, nor did it have a disk drive or any other way to interact with the data other than via the

network cable that connected it to the main frame.

3. "Therapist says children who view TV violence tend to become violent," Deseret News, Mar. 24 1989, 2B.

4. Christine Van De Velde, "The Power of Social Modeling: The Effects of Television Violence," http://www.stanford.edu/dept/bingschool/rsrchart/bandura.htm.

5. http://www.fcc.gov/ed/oip/FAQ.html#TheLaw, Feb. 2008.

6. Ibid.

7. Ibid.

8. With the switch to digital TV in 2009, this becomes even more of an issue, as current projections seem to indicate that many households have switched to cable or satellite rather than purchasing a digital converter box.

13
NONTECHNICAL
SOLUTIONS

"In its simplest terms, self-mastery is doing those things we should do and not doing those things we should not do. It requires strength, willpower, and honesty. As the traffic on the communications highway becomes a parking lot, we must depend more and more on our own personal moral filters to separate the good from the bad. Marvelous as it is in many ways, there is something hypnotic about using the Internet. I refer specifically to spending endless time in chat rooms or visiting the pornography sites."[1]

James E. Faust

Technology Alone Won't Solve the Problem

While there are many technical tools available to help, as we have seen in the previous chapters, none of them take the place of simply being involved in your children's online world. You need to know what they are doing, who they are interacting with, and where they are spending their time. Technology can help, but it will only take you so far. Those who truly want to access inappropriate content are going to do so, whether it is by browsing the Internet, watching television, playing games, finding videos on peer-to-peer applications, or through some other means. Young children will unknowingly put themselves into harm's way by being too trusting online and falling into the traps laid by online predators and malicious software creators. Only by opening the lines of communication and knowing where they spend their time and who they spend it with, will you be able to help your children navigate the dangerous waters of today's digital world.

Watch for the warning signs of addiction. Be tuned in to your children's lives—be aware of when they are spending too much time on the computer or becoming more withdrawn from family activities. Be aware of their sleep habits, and lock down the computer during the nighttime hours. Be conscious of their mood swings and know whether they are distancing themselves from their real-world friends.

10 SUGGESTIONS

Apart from the technologies we can employ, here are 10 simple suggestions you can implement to help keep your children safe while they are online

1. **Educate yourself about your computer and how the Internet works.** If parents know the dangers, this sets an example for the child to understand them as well. For example, instant messaging is an easy, cost-effective way to communicate with family and close friends, but care must be given to ensure that we only instant message people we already know, and we need to teach our children to stay away from public chat rooms. Such places present an unnecessary risk for children and adults. Simply banning a child from certain websites may only motivate them to become curious and to seek them out; whereas educating your child on how to keep safe will help them to understand the reasons that we want to limit their online experiences, and will help them develop their own "internal filter" so they can know on their own when they are venturing too far.

2. **Teach children to protect their identities while online.** Help your children understand how to safely share photos of themselves on their social networking sites, using the privacy settings to help protect these images from strangers. Teach them not to give out their names, addresses, phone numbers, schools, or other personal information where strangers can find them. Teach children not to share *any* personal information online without parental knowledge and permission. Help them understand that many predators pose

as children to gain access and information.

3. **Install a filtering program and learn its features and how to use it.** Family safety software is becoming extremely advanced and is an effective way to filter dangerous content. Additionally, this software usually comes with tools like time management, remote monitoring and reporting, and keystroke recognition. Good filtering programs allow you to view a history of the sites and chat rooms which have been visited and when the visits occured, as well as a record of incoming and outgoing emails and chat logs. Educate yourself about the latest filtering and family safety programs at sites such as www.internetfilterreview.com.

4. **Know the dangers associated with the applications and websites that your children use.** Teach family members to never open email from someone they don't know and to be wary of attachments to emails. Become familiar with the social networking sites your family members frequent, and be sure you know what people on your children's favorite sites are doing that could put your children in harm's way.

5. **Teach children what to do if they encounter pornography on a home or public computer, such as at a school or a library.** Just like we teach our children to "stop, drop, and roll" in a fire, you can teach children to quickly turn off power to the computer monitor and go get an adult. This can prevent a child from attempting to close the browser, which could potentially make the situation worse and expose him to more pornographic content.

6. **Manage your children's time on the Internet.** Scheduling times when a child can be on the Internet and the length of time he can be online ensures that you know when he is on the Internet and for how long. Not allowing him to have free reign reduces his chance of being exposed to inappropriate content. Be aware of what your children's school and public library policies are regarding Internet use and accessibility.

7. **Set specific Internet guidelines for your children to live by and consistently enforce consequences if your guidelines are not followed.** Giving your children specific guidelines to follow helps them know where they stand when it comes to how they should use the Internet as well as the consequences when they breach the rules. If a parent enforces consequences consistently, his children

will be more likely to follow the rules.

8. **Place computers in high-traffic areas of the home.** With PCs in the open, children will be less inclined to view and access material that may not be acceptable. Kitchens, family rooms, and studies tend to be good options because these rooms usually don't have doors and are typically less secluded than bedrooms. Position computer monitors so the screen faces out for public view. If you are having a tough time figuring out where to place your computer, look for where the carpet is the most warn in your home—that is a high-traffic area and may be an ideal location for a computer.

9. **Strive for open relationships with your children that would be conducive to open communication.** Open communication and trust are key when dealing with online safety. When children know what is expected from them and that their safety is a top priority, they will feel that if something happens—whether they are approached by a cyber stranger or bully or receive an inappropriate email—they can tell a parent and resolve the issue without being made to feel like they are in trouble.

10. **Teach children to tell a parent if they encounter any form of inappropriate content online.** This may include pornography, sexual solicitations, or online bullying. Teaching children to bring this to your attention will help reduce the fear or shame that accompanies accidental exposure. It also serves to open discussion about the dangers of pornography.

INTERNET PRIVACY POLICIES

There are laws and regulations that websites must follow with regard to maintaining privacy. It is important to understand Internet privacy policies and how they apply to your child. According to the FTC,[2] parents should be aware of the following items as they pertain to protecting a child's privacy on the Web. Website operators must:

Post Their Privacy Policies

Websites created for children or that knowingly collect information from kids under thirteen must post a notice of their information collection practices that includes:

> ➤ Types of personal information they collect from kids, for example,

name, home address, email address, or hobbies.

➤ How the site uses the information, for example, to market to the child who supplied the information, to notify contest winners, or to make the information available through a child's participation in a chat room.

➤ Whether personal information is forwarded to advertisers or other third parties.

➤ A contact at the site.

Get Parental Consent

In many cases, a site must obtain parental consent before collecting, using, or disclosing personal information about a child.

Consent is not required when a site is collecting an email address to:

➤ Respond to a one-time request from a child
➤ Provide notice to a parent
➤ Ensure the safety of a child on the site
➤ Send a newsletter or other information on a regular basis, as long as the site notifies a parent and gives them a chance to say no to the arrangement

Parents' responsibilities include the following:

Look for a Privacy Policy on Any Website Created for Children

The policy must be available through a link on the website's home page and on each page where personal information is collected. Websites for general audiences that have a children's section must post the notice on the home page of the section for children.

Read the policy closely to learn the kinds of personal information being collected, how the information will be used, and whether the information will be passed on to third parties. If you find a website that doesn't post basic protections for children's personal information, ask for details about their information collection practices.

Decide Whether to Give Consent

Giving consent authorizes the website to collect personal information from your child. You can give consent and still say no to having your child's information passed along to a third party.

Your consent isn't necessary if the website is collecting your child's email address simply to respond to a one-time request from your child.

OTHER RESOURCES

There are many online resources available for parents as they strive to keep their children safe in today's digital world. I will list only a few here, but you should know that there are many people who are dedicated to educating parents and families about how to remain safe while still making use of the technology that is available at our fingertips.

CommonSenseMedia.org is a great place to find information about much of the media today, from movies to television to games. They have a "Parent Advice" section of the website where they provide tips, advice, and references to help parents wade through the barrage of media that is in front of our children every day.

Enough.org and **CP80.org** are both organizations dedicated to making the Internet safer for children and families. Both have current statistics about the problems, suggestions on how to get involved, and updates on current legislation to protect our children such as the Child Online Protect Act and other international, federal, and state legislative efforts.

FocusOnTheFamily.com is Dr. James Dobson's website and is dedicated to strengthening families. There is a section on this website under "Parenting, Protecting Your Family" where they discuss issues related to online protection and Internet Safety.

FamilySafetyWiki.net is a website operated by the Church of Jesus Christ of Latter-Day Saints, which is dedicated to Family Safety topics. People from all over the world, whether members of the LDS Church or not, can collaborate on this site and provide up-to-date information on different issues relating to using technology safely in our homes.

iKeepSafe.org (Internet Keep Safe Coalition) is a wonderful organization founded by Jacalyn S. Leavitt, former First Lady of Utah, for the purpose of educating parents and children about the healthy use of technology and the Internet. They have content aimed at children and parents alike. Their site is a great source of material for instructing your children about how to remain safe on the Internet. Among other things, the iKeepSafe.org website contains three "parent rules" for safety on the Internet. These rules provide a simple, easy to remember process for keeping our children safe, regardless of the technology they are using. These rules are: keep current, keep communicating, and keep checking. Further explanation of these rules can be found at iKeepSafe.org or in the foreword to this book. Following these three simple steps will help you ensure that your children are kept safe, and that you know where they are going and what they are doing.

There are other organizations dedicated to educating parents and children and providing tips and advice regarding safe technology usage. Make use of these resources, keep yourself educated about technology, and maintain open communication with your children regarding their use of technology and you will be on the path to maintaining safe use of technology in your family.

Notes

1. James E. Faust, "The Power of Self-Mastery," *Ensign,* May 2000, 43.

2. www.ftc.gov/bcp/conline/pubs/online/kidspivacy.shtm.

14
WHAT NOW?

"Parents are never failures when they do their best to love, teach, pray, and care for their children. Their faith, prayers, and efforts will be consecrated to the good of their children."[1]

Robert D. Hales

CROSSROADS

We have covered a lot of ground in this book. We have learned about the dangers that exist in the virtual world and some tips about what you can do to create a safer environment for your children. Now, what will you do with this information?

Every family is different, and parents need to decide how involved they will get with their children's online activities. Some parents are much more concerned about not invading their children's privacy, and others are very comfortable with the concept. So where do we draw the line between being a good parent and being "big brother" when it comes to digital content? There are as many opinions on that subject as there are parents. Many blogs are dedicated to this subject, and it is clear from the comments posted on those blogs that a significant difference of opinion exists regarding how to help our children safely navigate the Internet.

Of particular interest are some of the comments that were left on the Microsoft blog when they announced that Parental Controls would be part of Windows Vista.[2] Based on these comments, some would have us believe that *any* attempt to monitor what our children do online, much less actually stop them from doing it, is a criminal offense. Personally, I wonder if the parents of children who have been abducted by Internet predators, or those whose children have committed suicide because of cyber bullying would agree. The bottom line is that this is a very personal decision that all parents need to make for their families. In the end, there is no silver bullet that is going to keep our children safe, so every parent needs to decide where their responsibilities lie as the guardians of their children in this digital world.

The Internet is indeed a dangerous place, but then so is our own backyard. In the very recent past, there was a case in Utah where a young girl walked into her backyard and was lured into the home of a neighbor who almost immediately killed her.[3] Even more recently, another young girl was killed when she went to a neighbor's apartment to play.[4] So do we stop our children from leaving the house? Of course not, but I guarantee that any parent who saw either of these stories certainly thought twice about letting their children play outside for a few days afterward.

So where are we on the continuum of Internet freedom with regard to our children? There are certainly many very good things that children can experience on the Internet, as well as some mindless, time-wasting opportunities (my kids have recently discovered Runescape and World of Warcraft). However, there are also some very bad areas of the Internet that our children can inadvertently wander into, or even worse, search out. As we saw in Chapter 7, even when we apply the safe search when using popular search engines, inappropriate content can still appear. If we are to help our children stay safe, we cannot let our guard down—just like we would not let down our guard while allowing our children to play near a busy street. The Internet is the "busy street" of the digital world, and even when we believe we have erected a safety fence around their play area, we need to be vigilant regarding their Internet usage.

Technology is far from perfect, and there are people who work hard every day to find ways to get their content in front of our children, circumventing the technology that we put in place to prevent it. So what do we do? Do we turn off the Internet in our homes? Do we monitor their activity, allow them to be exposed, and talk to them after-the-fact, or do we actively block access to the "bad" areas of the Internet? Personally, I believe that we are not fulfilling our responsibility as parents if we do not put some technological restrictions on our children's Internet access. This is a safety precaution no different from requiring our children to wear seatbelts or telling them not to talk to strangers

However, as I said above: technology isn't perfect. Filters will not catch everything, safe search will allow bad things through, and monitoring software will miss some things. So, it still comes down to us. We need to keep computers out of bedrooms, we need to teach our children[5] not to share personal information over the Internet, we need to teach them how to safely use email, and we need to be vigilant about knowing how they spend their time online and who they spend it with. And finally we need to follow-up with them regularly to ensure that they are following the rules.

If we rely too heavily on technology to protect them from the dangers of the Internet, we will find ourselves dealing with some issues that we had hoped to avoid. Doing nothing is not an option. Installing monitoring or filtering technology and then assuming you are protected is not responsible. It is sad that we have to discuss these things, but the bottom line is that having the Internet in our homes requires that we take action to ensure it is handled responsibly, and doing so requires that we do more than just throw technology at the problem.

A DANGEROUS COMBINATION:
AVAILABILITY, ACCESSIBILITY, AND ANONYMITY[6]

As we wrap up our discussion regarding family safety in this digital world, let me leave you with one final, very powerful, concept. There are three things that together cause a "perfect storm" of danger for our children. A friend of mine calls them the three As, namely: **Availability**, **Accessibility**, and **Anonymity**. These are the drivers of addictive behaviors—especially those addictions that one might be looked down upon for being involved in. These three As are the reason behind the growth of the porn industry through video recording technology as discussed in Chapter 2. These three As are the driving force behind the explosion of pornography on the Internet today. They are the driving force behind teenagers smoking behind the building or drinking out in the woods. The items they are seeking are available and accessible (sometimes through a friend who is old enough to purchase them or sometimes they are accessible in the home) and hiding behind the building, in the woods, or wherever else provides them with the anonymity that they need to feel comfortable that they won't get caught.

When something is widely available, easily accessible, and if one can access it anonymously, there is a very real danger of entanglement. In today's world, this applies to pornography, online gambling, and even gaming and chat rooms. Have you ever noticed that it is much easier to be bold, direct, and confrontational in a chat room, a text message, or an email message? That is because the computer adds a certain amount of anonymity. We are almost encouraged to talk in ways that we might not normally talk. Add to that the ability to hide behind a screen name, where the receiver may not be able to connect the words to us at all and we become even more emboldened. Think also of how much pornography is accessed when the individual believes he won't be caught, or when he thinks he won't be recognized. If he can do it anonymously, he is more likely to take the first step toward addiction.

As parents, we may not be able to do much about the availability of these things; they are going to continue to be available on the Internet as long as there are people out there trying to make a buck. However, we do have some control over how accessible we make these things within our homes—this is where technology can help. Filters, monitors, and time controls can help limit the accessibility of addicting online content in our homes. But the thing we have the most control over is the anonymity. We need to ensure that our children know that we will be watching over them—not as "big brother," but as caring, loving parents. They need to understand that there is no expectation of privacy when they are using any of the computers in our home—for them or for their friends. They need to know that we will be asking them questions about what they are doing online—specific questions. They need to know that we will be their "friend" in their social networking environments, and that we will be watching what they post for their online friends to see. Removing the anonymity from their online activities will go a long way toward helping to keep them safe.

PARENTING IN A DIGITAL WORLD

I hope this book has provided specific, practical suggestions you can use to protect your family members while still allowing them to be part of this grand new digital world in which we live. Remember that technology changes quickly, and it is likely that many of the technical suggestions in this book will soon be dated. In my opinion, the most important chapter in this book is Chapter 13, in which we discussed the nontechnical solutions to these problems. Protecting our families in this digital world is not about throwing more technology at them, nor is there a "set it and forget it" solution. The real answer is to help our children develop their own, internal filters that will help them understand what is appropriate when using technology and when to turn and run instead of staying and looking. The real answer is to find a way to limit the accessibility of addicting content in our homes and the anonymity that our children feel when accessing it digitally. Parenting in the digital world means getting involved in our children's online lives, knowing where they are going and what they are doing, and making sure that they know we love and care for them—both in the real world and in the virtual one.

Notes

1. Robert D. Hales, "With All the Feeling of A Tender Parent: A message of Hope to Families," *Liahona*, May 2004, 88–91.
2. See http://blogs.msdn.com/ie/archive/2006/03/01/54169.aspx.
3. "Destiny Norton Found Dead, Suspect Arrested," July 25, 2006, http://www.ksl.com/?nid=148&sid+380101
4. "Man Charged With Murdering Hser Ner Moo," April 8,2008, http://deseretnews.com/article/1,5143,695268555,00.html.
5. See http://child-internet-safety.com/safety.php.
6. Adapted from Dr. Alvin Cooper's "*Triple A Engine Effect*": Access, Affordability, and Anonymity.

ABOUT THE AUTHOR

Ken is a strong technology leader with experience in software development, architecture, software design, program management, project management, quality assurance, and user interaction. During the course of more than twenty years in the industry, he has worked as a software tester, software developer, enterprise architect, manager, director, VP, and C-level executive. He held the position of CTO at two different security-related companies and was responsible for all internal and external IT-related functions within those organizations and was a key member of the strategy team for the overall company direction.

Ken holds three U.S. patents for his work on enterprise security and anti-virus technology and published his unique development ideas and concepts regarding component-oriented plug-and-play software before it was popular in the industry. As CTO, he worked very closely with, and delivered solutions to, the CIA, FBI, Secret Service, and Department of Homeland Security, as well as their equivalent organizations in other countries. He is a highly effective leader who is known for motivating employees to achieve success and for improving quality and timeliness of deliverables.

Throughout his career, Ken has led organizations at WordPerfect, Novell, Intel, Relizon, AccessData, ContentWatch, and the LDS Church. He participated in the design, development, and/or release of multiple award-winning products, such as: WordPerfect for Windows; PerfectOffice; LANDesk Management Suite; Symantec AntiVirus, Corporate Edition; RegistryViewer; Password Recovery Toolkit; and Forensic Toolkit.

Ken holds a Bachelor's of Science in Computer Science and Information Systems from Utah Valley University and a Masters of Business Administration from Brigham Young University.